Workers of All Countries, Unite!

MARX and ENGELS
Through the Eyes
of Their Contemporaries

Progress Publishers
Moscow

PUBLISHERS' NOTE

This collection is an abridged version of the *Reminiscences of Marx and Engels* published in English by the Foreign Languages Publishing House, Moscow.

РАССКАЗЫ О МАРКСЕ И ЭНГЕЛЬСЕ

На английском языке

First printing 1972

Printed in the Union of Soviet Socialist Republics

CONTENTS

	Page
Frederick Engels. Speech at the Graveside of Karl Marx	5
V. I. Lenin. Karl Marx	8
V. I. Lenin. Frederick Engels	13
Paul Lafargue. Reminiscences of Marx	22
Paul Lafargue. Reminiscences of Engels	40
Wilhelm Liebknecht. Reminiscences of Marx	48
1. First Meeting with Marx	49
2. First Conversation	49
3. Marx, Teacher and Educator of Revolutionaries	52
4. Marx's Style	56
5. Marx the Politician, Scientist and Man	58
6. Marx at Work	62
7. In the House in Dean Street	64
8. Emigrants' Intrigues	65
9. Meetings at Marx's	66
10. Marx and Children	69
11. Lenchen	72
12. Walks with Marx	73
13. An Unpleasant Quarter of an Hour	77
14. Marx and Chess	80
15. Privation and Hardship	82
16. Illness and Death of Marx	82
17. Marx's Grave	87
18. Seeking Out Places of Old	90
Wilhelm Liebknecht. Reminiscences of Engels	95
Friedrich Lessner. Before 1848 and After	100
Friedrich Lessner. A Worker's Reminiscences of Frederick Engels	115
Friedrich Adolf Sorge. On Marx	124
H. A. Lopatin. From a Letter to N. P. Sinelnikov	128
Jenny Marx. Short Sketch of an Eventful Life	131
Jenny Marx to Joseph Weydemeyer	143

Jenny Marx to Luise Weydemeyer	147
Eleanor Marx-Aveling. Karl Marx	153
Eleanor Marx-Aveling. Frederick Engels	160
Edgar Longuet. Some Aspects of Karl Marx's Family Life	170
Poverty of the Emigrants in London	173
A Prodigious Life of Work and Struggle	175
Confessions	179
Franzisca Kugelmann. Small Traits of Marx's Great Character	180
N. Morozov. Visits to Karl Marx	193
Edward Aveling, Dr. Sc. Engels at Home	196
Fanni Kravchinskaya. Reminiscences	203

Frederick Engels

SPEECH AT THE GRAVESIDE OF KARL MARX

On the 14th of March, at a quarter to three in the afternoon, the greatest living thinker ceased to think. He had been left alone for scarcely two minutes, and when we came back we found him in his armchair, peacefully gone to sleep —but for ever.

An immeasurable loss has been sustained both by the militant proletariat of Europe and America, and by historical science, in the death of this man. The gap that has been left by the departure of this mighty spirit will soon enough make itself felt.

Just as Darwin discovered the law of development of organic nature, so Marx discovered the law of development of human history: the simple fact, hitherto concealed by an overgrowth of ideology, that mankind must first of all eat, drink, have shelter and clothing, before it can pursue politics, science, art, religion, etc.; that therefore the production of the immediate material means of subsistence and consequently the degree of economic development attained by a given people or during a given epoch form the foundation upon which the state institutions, the legal conceptions, art, and even the ideas on religion, of the people concerned have been evolved, and in the light of which they must, therefore, be explained, instead of *vice versa*, as had hitherto been the case.

But that is not all. Marx also discovered the special law of motion governing the present-day capitalist mode of production and the bourgeois society that this mode of production has created. The discovery of surplus value suddenly threw light on the problem, in trying to solve which all previous investigations, of both bourgeois economists and socialist critics, had been groping in the dark.

Two such discoveries would be enough for one lifetime. Happy the man to whom it is granted to make even one such discovery. But in every single field which Marx investigated—and he investigated very many fields, none of them superficially—in every field, even in that of mathematics, he made independent discoveries.

Such was the man of science. But this was not even half the man. Science was for Marx a historically dynamic, revolutionary force. However great the joy with which he welcomed a new discovery in some theoretical science whose practical application perhaps it was as yet quite impossible to envisage, he experienced quite another kind of joy when the discovery involved immediate revolutionary changes in industry, and in historical development in general. For example, he followed closely the development of the discoveries made in the field of electricity and recently those of Marcel Deprez.[1]

For Marx was before all else a revolutionist. His real mission in life was to contribute, in one way or another, to the overthrow of capitalist society and of the state institutions which it had brought into being, to contribute to the liberation of the modern proletariat, which *he* was the first to make conscious of its own position and its needs, conscious of the conditions of its emancipation. Fighting was his element. And he fought with a passion, a tenacity and a success such as few could rival. His work on the first *Rheinische Zeitung* (1842), the Paris *Vorwärts* (1844), the *Deutsche-Brüsseler-Zeitung* (1847), the *Neue Rheinische Zeitung* (1848-49), the *New York Tribune* (1852-61),[2] and in addition to these a host of militant pamphlets, work in organisations in Paris, Brussels and London, and finally, crowning all, the formation of the great International Work-

---

[1] *Deprez, Marcel* (1843-1918)—French physicist, author of the first experiments on distant transmission of electricity.—*Ed.*

[2] Marx was the editor of the *Rheinische Zeitung* and the *Neue Rheinische Zeitung*. As for the rest of the newspapers, he either contributed to them or took an active part in editing them.—*Ed.*

ing Men's Association[1]—this was indeed an achievement of which its founder might well have been proud even if he had done nothing else.

And, consequently, Marx was the best hated and most calumniated man of his time. Governments, both absolutist and republican, deported him from their territories. Bourgeois, whether conservative or ultra-democratic, vied with one another in heaping slanders upon him. All this he brushed aside as though it were cobweb, ignoring it, answering only when extreme necessity compelled him. And he died beloved, revered and mourned by millions of revolutionary fellow workers—from the mines of Siberia to California, in all parts of Europe and America—and I make bold to say that though he may have had many opponents he had hardly one personal enemy.

His name will endure through the ages, and so also will his work!

March 17, 1883

---

[1] The International Working Men's Association (First International) was founded by Marx in 1864 and existed until 1872. It was the embryo of a proletarian party.—*Ed.*

V. I. Lenin

KARL MARX[1]

Marx, Karl, was born on May 5, 1818 (New Style), in the city of Trier (Rhenish Prussia). His father was a lawyer, a Jew, who in 1824 adopted Protestantism. The family was well-to-do, cultured, but not revolutionary. After graduating from a *Gymnasium* in Trier, Marx entered the university, first at Bonn and later in Berlin, where he read law, majoring in history and philosophy. He concluded his university course in 1841, submitting a doctoral thesis on the philosophy of Epicurus.[2] At the time Marx was a Hegelian idealist in his views. In Berlin, he belonged to the circle of "Left Hegelians" (Bruno Bauer and others) who sought to draw atheistic and revolutionary conclusions from Hegel's[3] philosophy.

After graduating, Marx moved to Bonn, hoping to become a professor. However, the reactionary policy of the government, which deprived Ludwig Feuerbach of his chair in 1832, refused to allow him to return to the university in 1836, and in 1841 forbade young Professor Bruno Bauer to lecture at Bonn, made Marx abandon the idea of an academic career. Left Hegelian views were making rapid

---

[1] Only the part of Lenin's article containing biographical data on Marx is printed here.—*Ed.*

[2] *Epicurus* (c. 341-270 B.C.)—famous Greek materialist philosopher, atheist.—*Ed.*

[3] *Hegel, Georg Wilhelm* (1770-1831)—great German philosopher, objective idealist; gave most thorough analysis of idealist dialectics.—*Ed.*

headway in Germany at the time. Ludwig Feuerbach began to criticise theology, particularly after 1836, and turn to materialism, which in 1841 gained the ascendancy in his philosophy (*The Essence of Christianity*). The year 1843 saw the appearance of his *Principles of the Philosophy of the Future*. "One must oneself have experienced the liberating effect" of these books, Engels subsequently wrote of these works of Feuerbach. "We [i.e., the Left Hegelians, including Marx] all became at once Feuerbachians." At that time, some radical bourgeois in the Rhineland, who were in touch with the Left Hegelians, founded, in Cologne, an opposition paper called *Rheinische Zeitung* (the first issue appeared on January 1, 1842). Marx and Bruno Bauer were invited to be the chief contributors, and in October 1842 Marx became editor-in-chief and moved from Bonn to Cologne. The newspaper's revolutionary-democratic trend became more and more pronounced under Marx's editorship, and the government first imposed double and triple censorship on the paper, and then on January 1, 1843, decided to suppress it. Marx had to resign the editorship before that date, but his resignation did not save the paper, which suspended publication in March 1843. Of the major articles Marx contributed to the *Rheinische Zeitung*, Engels notes, in addition to those indicated below (see *Bibliography*[1]), an article on the condition of peasant vinegrowers in the Moselle Valley. Marx's journalistic activities convinced him that he was insufficiently acquainted with political economy, and he zealously set out to study it.

In 1843, Marx married, at Kreuznach, Jenny von Westphalen, a childhood friend he had become engaged to while still a student. His wife came of a reactionary family of the Prussian nobility, her elder brother being Prussia's Minister of the Interior during a most reactionary period—1850-58. In the autumn of 1843, Marx went to Paris in order to publish a radical journal abroad, together with Arnold Ruge (1802-1880; Left Hegelian; in prison in 1825-30; a political exile following 1848, and a Bismarckian after 1866-70). Only one issue of this journal, *Deutsch-Französische Jahr-*

---

[1] At the end of this article, which was written in 1914 for the Granat Encyclopaedia, Lenin gave a survey of literature of Marxism and on Marxism which is here omitted.—*Ed.*

bücher, appeared; publication was discontinued owing to the difficulty of secretly distributing it in Germany, and to disagreement with Ruge. Marx's articles in this journal showed that he was already a revolutionary, who advocated "merciless criticism of everything existing", and in particular the "criticism by weapon", and appealed to the *masses* and to the *proletariat*.

In September 1844 Frederick Engels came to Paris for a few days, and from that time on became Marx's closest friend. They both took a most active part in the then seething life of the revolutionary groups in Paris (of particular importance at the time was Proudhon's doctrine, which Marx pulled to pieces in his *Poverty of Philosophy*, 1847); waging a vigorous struggle against the various doctrines of petty-bourgeois socialism, they worked out the theory and tactics of revolutionary *proletarian socialism*, or communism (Marxism). See Marx's works of this period, 1844-48, in the *Bibliography*. At the insistent request of the Prussian Government, Marx was banished from Paris in 1845, as a dangerous revolutionary. He went to Brussels. In the spring of 1847 Marx and Engels joined a secret propaganda society called the Communist League; they took a prominent part in the League's Second Congress (London, November 1847), at whose request they drew up the celebrated *Communist Manifesto*, which appeared in February 1848. With the clarity and brilliance of genius, this work outlines a new world-conception, consistent materialism, which also embraces the realm of social life; dialectics, as the most comprehensive and profound doctrine of development; the theory of the class struggle and of the world-historic revolutionary role of the proletariat—the creator of a new, communist society.

On the outbreak of the Revolution of February 1848, Marx was banished from Belgium. He returned to Paris, whence, after the March Revolution, he went to Cologne, Germany, where the *Neue Rheinische Zeitung* was published from June 1, 1848 to May 19, 1849, with Marx as editor-in-chief. The new theory was splendidly confirmed by the course of the revolutionary events of 1848-49, just as it has been subsequently confirmed by all proletarian and democratic movements in all countries of the world. The victorious counter-revolutionaries first instigated court proceedings against Marx (he was acquitted on February 9, 1849), and then banished him from Germany (May 16, 1849). First Marx went to Paris, was again banished after the demonstration of June 13, 1849, and then went to London, where he lived till his death.

His life as a political exile was a very hard one, as the correspondence between Marx and Engels (published in 1913) clearly reveals. Poverty weighed heavily on Marx and his family; had it not been for Engels' constant and selfless financial aid, Marx would not only have been unable to complete *Capital* but would have inevitably been crushed by want. Moreover, the prevailing doctrines and trends of petty-bourgeois socialism, and of non-proletarian socialism in general, forced Marx to wage a continuous and merciless struggle and sometimes to repeal the most savage and monstrous personal attacks (*Herr Vogt*[1]). Marx, who stood aloof from circles of political exiles, developed his materialist theory in a number of historical works (see *Bibliography*), devoting himself mainly to a study of political economy. Marx revolutionised this science (see "The Marxist Doctrine", below) in his *Contribution to the Critique of Political Economy* (1859) and *Capital* (Vol. I, 1867).

The revival of the democratic movements in the late fifties and in the sixties recalled Marx to practical activity. In 1864 (September 28) the International Working Men's Association—the celebrated First International—was founded in London. Marx was the heart and soul of this organisation, and author of its first Address and of a host of resolutions, declarations and manifestos. In uniting the labour movement of various countries, striving to channel into joint activity the various forms of non-proletarian, pre-Marxist socialism (Mazzini, Proudhon, Bakunin, liberal trade-unionism in Britain, Lassallean vacillations to the right in Germany, etc.), and in combating the theories of all these sects and schools, Marx hammered out a uniform tactic for the proletarian struggle of the working class in the various countries. Following the downfall of the Paris Commune (1871)—of which Marx gave such a profound, clear-cut, brilliant, *effective* and revolutionary analysis (*The*

---

[1] *Herr Vogt*—a pamphlet written by Marx against Karl Vogt, a German bourgeois democrat.—*Ed.*

Civil War in France, 1871)—and the Bakuninist-caused cleavage in the International, the latter organisation could no longer exist in Europe. After the Hague Congress of the International (1872), Marx had the General Council of the International transferred to New York. The First International had played its historical part, and now made way for a period of a far greater development of the labour movement in all countries in the world, a period in which the movement grew in *scope*, and *mass* socialist working-class parties in individual national states were formed.

Marx's health was undermined by his strenuous work in the International and his still more strenuous theoretical occupations. He continued work on the refashioning of political economy and on the completion of *Capital*, for which he collected a mass of new material and studied a number of languages (Russian, for instance). However, ill-health prevented him from completing *Capital*.

His wife died on December 2, 1881, and on March 14, 1883, Marx passed away peacefully in his armchair. He lies buried next to his wife at Highgate Cemetery in London. Of Marx's children some died in childhood in London, when the family were living in destitute circumstances. Three daughters married English and French socialists: Eleanor Aveling, Laura Lafargue and Jenny Longuet. The latter's son is a member of the French Socialist Party.

V. I. Lenin

FREDERICK ENGELS

> What a torch of reason ceased to burn,
> What a heart has ceased to beat![1]

On August 5 (New Style), 1895, Frederick Engels died in London. After his friend Karl Marx (who died in 1883), Engels was the finest scholar and teacher of the modern proletariat in the whole civilised world. From the time that fate brought Karl Marx and Frederick Engels together, the two friends devoted their life's work to a common cause. And so to understand what Frederick Engels has done for the proletariat, one must have a clear idea of the significance of Marx's teaching and work for the development of the contemporary working-class movement. Marx and Engels were the first to show that the working class and its demands are a necessary outcome of the present economic system, which together with the bourgeoisie inevitably creates and organises the proletariat. They showed that it is not the well-meaning efforts of noble-minded individuals, but the class struggle of the organised proletariat that will deliver humanity from the evils which now oppress it. In their scientific works, Marx and Engels were the first to explain that socialism is not the invention of dreamers, but the final aim and necessary result of the development of the productive forces in modern society. All recorded history hitherto has been a history of class struggle, of the succession of the rule and victory of certain social classes over others. And this will continue until the foundations of class struggle

---

[1] From N. A. Nekrasov's poem "In Memory of Dobrolyubov".—*Ed.*

and of class domination—private property and anarchic social production—disappear. The interests of the proletariat demand the destruction of these foundations, and therefore the conscious class struggle of the organised workers must be directed against them. And every class struggle is a political struggle.

These views of Marx and Engels have now been adopted by all proletarians who are fighting for their emancipation. But when in the forties the two friends took part in the socialist literature and the social movements of their time, they were absolutely novel. There were then many people, talented and without talent, honest and dishonest, who, absorbed in the struggle for political freedom, in the struggle against the despotism of kings, police and priests, failed to observe the antagonism between the interests of the bourgeoisie and those of the proletariat. These people would not entertain the idea of the workers acting as an independent social force. On the other hand, there were many dreamers, some of them geniuses, who thought that it was only necessary to convince the rulers and the governing classes of the injustice of the contemporary social order, and it would then be easy to establish peace and general well-being on earth. They dreamt of a socialism without struggle. Lastly, nearly all the socialists of that time and the friends of the working class generally regarded the proletariat only as an *ulcer*, and observed with horror how it grew with the growth of industry. They all, therefore, sought for a means to stop the development of industry and of the proletariat, to stop the "wheel of history". Marx and Engels did not share the general fear of the development of the proletariat; on the contrary, they placed all their hopes on its continued growth. The more proletarians there are, the greater is their strength as a revolutionary class, and the nearer and more possible does socialism become. The services rendered by Marx and Engels to the working class may be expressed in a few words thus: they taught the working class to know itself and be conscious of itself, and they substituted science for dreams.

That is why the name and life of Engels should be known to every worker. That is why in this collection of articles, the aim of which, as of all our publications, is to awaken class-consciousness in the Russian workers, we must give a sketch of the life and work of Frederick Engels, one of the two great teachers of the modern proletariat.

Engels was born in 1820 in Barmen, in the Rhine Province of the kingdom of Prussia. His father was a manufacturer. In 1838 Engels, without having completed his high-school studies, was forced by family circumstances to enter a commercial house in Bremen as a clerk. Commercial affairs did not prevent Engels from pursuing his scientific and political education. He had come to hate autocracy and the tyranny of bureaucrats while still at high school. The study of philosophy led him further. At that time Hegel's teaching dominated German philosophy, and Engels became his follower. Although Hegel himself was an admirer of the autocratic Prussian state, in whose service he was as a professor at Berlin University, Hegel's *teachings* were revolutionary. Hegel's faith in human reason and its rights, and the fundamental thesis of Hegelian philosophy that the universe is undergoing a constant process of change and development, led some of the disciples of the Berlin philosopher—those who refused to accept the existing situation—to the idea that the struggle against this situation, the struggle against existing wrong and prevalent evil, is also rooted in the universal law of eternal development. If all things develop, if institutions of one kind give place to others, why should the autocracy of the Prussian king or of the Russian tsar, the enrichment of an insignificant minority at the expense of the vast majority, or the domination of the bourgeoisie over the people, continue for ever? Hegel's philosophy spoke of the development of the mind and of ideas; it was *idealistic*. From the development of the mind it deduced the development of nature, of man, and of human, social relations. While retaining Hegel's idea of the eternal process of development,[1] Marx and Engels rejected the preconceived idealist view; turning to life, they saw that it is not the development of mind that explains the development of nature but that, on the contrary, the explanation of mind must be derived from nature, from matter....

---

[1] Marx and Engels frequently pointed out that in their intellectual development they were much indebted to the great German philosophers, particularly to Hegel. "Without German philosophy," Engels says, "scientific socialism would never have come into being." (*Note by Lenin.—Ed.*)

Unlike Hegel and the other Hegelians, Marx and Engels were materialists. Regarding the world and humanity materialistically, they perceived that just as material causes underlie all natural phenomena, so the development of human society is conditioned by the development of material forces, the productive forces. On the development of the productive forces depend the relations into which men enter with one another in the production of the things required for the satisfaction of human needs. And in these relations lies the explanation of all the phenomena of social life, human aspirations, ideas and laws. The development of the productive forces creates social relations based upon private property, but now we see that this same development of the productive forces deprives the majority of their property and concentrates it in the hands of an insignificant minority. It abolishes property, the basis of the modern social order, it itself strives towards the very aim which the socialists have set themselves. All the socialists have to do is to realise which social force, owing to its position in modern society, is interested in bringing socialism about, and to impart to this force the consciousness of its interests and of its historical task. This force is the proletariat. Engels got to know the proletariat in England, in the centre of English industry, Manchester, where he settled in 1842, entering the service of a commercial firm of which his father was a shareholder. Here Engels not only sat in the factory office but wandered about the slums in which the workers were cooped up, and saw their poverty and misery with his own eyes. But he did not confine himself to personal observations. He read all that had been revealed before him about the condition of the British working class and carefully studied all the official documents he could lay his hands on. The fruit of these studies and observations was the book which appeared in 1845: *The Condition of the Working Class in England*. We have already mentioned what was the chief service rendered by Engels in writing *The Condition of the Working Class in England*. Even before Engels, many people had described the sufferings of the proletariat and had pointed to the necessity of helping it. Engels was the *first* to say that the proletariat is *not only* a suffering class; that it is, in fact, the disgraceful economic condition of the proletariat that drives it irresistibly forward and compels it to fight for its

Karl Marx. 1872

Frederick Engels. 1872

ultimate emancipation. And the fighting proletariat *will help itself*. The political movement of the working class will inevitably lead the workers to realise that their only salvation lies in socialism. On the other hand, socialism will become a force only when it becomes the aim of the *political* struggle of the working *class*. Such are the main ideas of Engels' book on the condition of the working class in England, ideas which have now been adopted by all thinking and fighting proletarians, but which at that time were entirely new. These ideas were set out in a book written in absorbing style and filled with most authentic and shocking pictures of the misery of the English proletariat. The book was a terrible indictment of capitalism and the bourgeoisie and created a profound impression. Engels' book began to be quoted everywhere as presenting the best picture of the condition of the modern proletariat. And, in fact, neither before 1845 nor after has there appeared so striking and truthful a picture of the misery of the working class.

It was not until he came to England that Engels became a socialist. In Manchester he established contacts with people active in the English labour movement at the time and began to write for English socialist publications. In 1844, while on his way back to Germany, he became acquainted in Paris with Marx, with whom he had already started to correspond. In Paris, under the influence of the French socialists and French life, Marx had also become a socialist. Here the friends jointly wrote a book entitled *The Holy Family, or Critique of Critical Criticism*. This book, which appeared a year before *The Condition of the Working Class in England*, and the greater part of which was written by Marx, contains the foundations of revolutionary materialist socialism, the main ideas of which we have expounded above. "The holy family" is a facetious nickname for the Bauer brothers, the philosophers, and their followers. These gentlemen preached a criticism which stood above all reality, above parties and politics, which rejected all practical activity, and which only "critically" contemplated the surrounding world and the events going on within it. These gentlemen, the Bauers, looked down on the proletariat as an uncritical mass. Marx and Engels vigorously opposed this absurd and harmful tendency. In the name of a real, human person—the worker, trampled down by the ruling classes and the state—they demanded, not contemplation, but a struggle for a better order of society. They, of course, regarded the proletariat as the force that is capable of waging this struggle and that is interested in it. Even before the appearance of *The Holy Family*, Engels had published in Marx's and Ruge's *Deutsch-Französische Jahrbücher* his "Critical Essays on Political Economy", in which he examined the principal phenomena of the contemporary economic order from a socialist standpoint, regarding them as necessary consequences of the rule of private property. Contact with Engels was undoubtedly a factor in Marx's decision to study political economy, the science in which his works have produced a veritable revolution.

From 1845 to 1847 Engels lived in Brussels and Paris, combining scientific work with practical activities among the German workers in Brussels and Paris. Here Marx and Engels established contact with the secret German Communist League, which commissioned them to expound the main principles of the socialism they had worked out. Thus arose the famous *Manifesto of the Communist Party* of Marx and Engels, published in 1848. This little booklet is worth whole volumes: to this day its spirit inspires and guides the entire organised and fighting proletariat of the civilised world.

The revolution of 1848, which broke out first in France and then spread to other West-European countries, brought Marx and Engels back to their native country. Here, in Rhenish Prussia, they took charge of the democratic *Neue Rheinische Zeitung* published in Cologne. The two friends were the heart and soul of all revolutionary-democratic aspirations in Rhenish Prussia. They fought to the last ditch in defence of freedom and of the interests of the people against the forces of reaction. The latter, as we know, gained the upper hand. The *Neue Rheinische Zeitung* was suppressed. Marx, who during his exile had lost his Prussian citizenship, was deported; Engels took part in the armed popular uprising, fought for liberty in three battles, and after the defeat of the rebels fled, via Switzerland, to London.

Marx also settled in London. Engels soon became a clerk again, and then a shareholder, in the Manchester commercial firm in which he had worked in the forties. Until 1870 he lived in Manchester, while Marx lived in London, but this did not prevent their maintaining a most lively interchange of ideas: they corresponded almost daily. In this correspondence the two friends exchanged views and discoveries and continued to collaborate in working out scientific socialism. In 1870 Engels moved to London, and their joint intellectual life, of the most strenuous nature, continued until 1883, when Marx died. Its fruit was, on Marx's side, *Capital*, the greatest work on political economy of our age, and on Engels' side, a number of works both large and small. Marx worked on the analysis of the complex phenomena of capitalist economy. Engels, in simply written works, often of a polemical character, dealt with more general scientific problems and with diverse phenomena of the past and present in the spirit of the materialist conception of history and Marx's economic theory. Of Engels' works we shall mention: the polemical work against Dühring (analysing highly important problems in the domain of philosophy, natural science and the social sciences),[1] *The Origin of the Family, Private Property and the State* (translated into Russian, published in St. Petersburg, 3rd ed., 1895), *Ludwig Feuerbach* (Russian translation and notes by G. Plekhanov, Geneva, 1892), an article on the foreign policy of the Russian Government (translated into Russian in the Geneva *Sotsial-Demokrat* Nos. 1 and 2), splendid articles on the housing question, and finally, two small but very valuable articles on Russia's economic development (*Frederick Engels on Russia*, translated into Russian by Zasulich, Geneva, 1894). Marx died before he could put the final touches to his vast work on capital. The draft, however, was already finished, and after the death of his friend, Engels undertook the onerous task of preparing and publishing the second and the third volumes of *Capital*. He published Volume II in 1885 and Volume III in 1894 (his death prevented the preparation of Volume IV). These two volumes entailed a vast amount of labour. Adler, the Austrian Social-Democrat, has rightly remarked that by publishing volumes II and III of *Capital* Engels erected a majestic monument to the

---

[1] This is a wonderfully rich and instructive book. Unfortunately, only a small portion of it, containing a historical outline of the development of socialism, has been translated into Russian (*The Development of Scientific Socialism*, 2nd ed., Geneva, 1892). (*Note by Lenin.* —*Ed.*)

genius who had been his friend, a monument on which, without intending it, he indelibly carved his own name. Indeed these two volumes of *Capital* are the work of two men: Marx and Engels. Old legends contain various moving instances of friendship. The European proletariat may say that its science was created by two scholars and fighters, whose relationship to each other surpasses the most moving stories of the ancients about human friendship. Engels always—and, on the whole, quite justly—placed himself after Marx. "In Marx's lifetime," he wrote to an old friend, "I played second fiddle." His love for the living Marx, and his reverence for the memory of the dead Marx were boundless. This stern fighter and austere thinker possessed a deeply loving soul.

After the movement of 1848-49, Marx and Engels in exile did not confine themselves to scientific research. In 1864 Marx founded the International Working Men's Association, and led this society for a whole decade. Engels also took an active part in its affairs. The work of the International Association, which, in accordance with Marx's idea, united proletarians of all countries, was of tremendous significance in the development of the working-class movement. But even with the closing down of the International Association in the seventies, the unifying role of Marx and Engels did not cease. On the contrary, it may be said that their importance as the spiritual leaders of the working-class movement grew continuously, because the movement itself grew uninterruptedly. After the death of Marx, Engels continued alone as the counsellor and leader of the European socialists. His advice and directions were sought for equally by the German socialists, whose strength, despite government persecution, grew rapidly and steadily, and by representatives of backward countries, such as the Spaniards, Rumanians and Russians, who were obliged to ponder and weigh their first steps. They all drew on the rich store of knowledge and experience of Engels in his old age.

Marx and Engels, who both knew Russian and read Russian books, took a lively interest in the country, followed the Russian revolutionary movement with sympathy and maintained contact with Russian revolutionaries. They both became socialists after being *democrats,* and the democratic feeling of *hatred* for political despotism was exceedingly strong in them. This direct political feeling, combined with a profound theoretical understanding of the connection between political despotism and economic oppression, and also their rich experience of life, made Marx and Engels uncommonly responsive *politically*. That is why the heroic struggle of the handful of Russian revolutionaries against the mighty tsarist government evoked a most sympathetic echo in the hearts of these tried revolutionaries. On the other hand, the tendency, for the sake of illusory economic advantages, to turn away from the most immediate and important task of the Russian socialists, namely, the winning of political freedom, naturally appeared suspicious to them and was even regarded by them as a direct betrayal of the great cause of the social revolution. "The emancipation of the workers must be the act of the working class itself"—Marx and Engels constantly taught. But in order to fight for its economic emancipation, the proletariat must win itself certain *political* rights. Moreover, Marx and Engels clearly saw that a political revolution in Russia would be of tremendous significance to the West-European working-class movement as well. Autocratic Russia had always been a bulwark of European reaction in general. The extraordinarily favourable international position enjoyed by Russia as a result of the war of 1870, which for a long time sowed discord between Germany and France, of course only enhanced the importance of autocratic Russia as a reactionary force. Only a free Russia, a Russia that had no need either to oppress the Poles, Finns, Germans, Armenians or any other small nations, or constantly to set France and Germany at loggerheads, would enable modern Europe, rid of the burden of war, to breathe freely, would weaken all the reactionary elements in Europe and strengthen the European working class. That was why Engels ardently desired the establishment of political freedom in Russia for the sake of the progress of the working-class movement in the West as well. In him the Russian revolutionaries have lost their best friend.

Let us always honour the memory of Frederick Engels, a great fighter and teacher of the proletariat!

Paul Lafargue

REMINISCENCES OF MARX[1]

> He was a man, take him for all in all,
> I shall not look upon his like again.
> (*Hamlet*, Act I, Sc. 2)

1

I met Karl Marx for the first time in February 1865. The First International had been founded on September 28, 1864 at a meeting in St. Martin's Hall, London, and I went to London from Paris to give Marx news of the development of the young organisation there. M. Tolain, now a senator in the bourgeois republic, gave me a letter of introduction.

I was then 24 years old. As long as I live I shall remember the impression that first visit made on me. Marx was not well at the time. He was working on the first book of *Capital*, which was not published until two years later, in 1867. He feared he would not be able to finish his work and was therefore glad of visits from young people. "I must train men to continue communist propaganda after me," he used to say.

Karl Marx was one of the rare men who could be leaders in science and public life at the same time: these two aspects were so closely united in him that one can understand him only by taking into account both the scholar and the socialist fighter.

Marx held the view that science must be pursued for itself, irrespective of the eventual results of research, but at the same time that a scientist could only debase himself by

---

[1] *Lafargue, Paul* (1842-1911)—prominent figure in the French and international working-class movement, friend and follower of Marx and Engels, husband of Marx's daughter, Laura.

These reminiscences were published in 1890.—*Ed.*

giving up active participation in public life or shutting himself up in his study or laboratory like a maggot in cheese and holding aloof from the life and political struggle of his contemporaries.

"Science must not be a selfish pleasure," he used to say. "Those who have the good fortune to be able to devote themselves to scientific pursuits must be the first to place their knowledge at the service of humanity." One of his favourite sayings was: "Work for humanity."

Although Marx sympathised profoundly with the sufferings of the working classes, it was not sentimental considerations but the study of history and political economy that led him to communist views. He maintained that any unbiased man, free from the influence of private interests and not blinded by class prejudices, must necessarily come to the same conclusions.

Yet while studying the economic and political development of human society without any preconceived opinion, Marx wrote with no other intention than to propagate the results of his research and with a determined will to provide a scientific basis for the socialist movement, which had so far been lost in the clouds of utopianism. He gave publicity to his views only to promote the triumph of the working class, whose historic mission is to establish communism as soon as it has achieved political and economic leadership of society....

Marx did not confine his activity to the country he was born in. "I am a citizen of the world," he used to say; "I am active wherever I am." And in fact, no matter what country events and political persecution drove him to—France, Belgium, England—he took a prominent part in the revolutionary movements which developed there.

However, it was not the untiring and incomparable socialist agitator but rather the scientist that I first saw in his study in Maitland Park Road. That study was the centre to which Party comrades came from all parts of the civilised world to find out the opinion of the master of socialist thought. One must know that historic room before one can penetrate into the intimacy of Marx's spiritual life.

It was on the first floor, flooded by light from a broad window that looked out on to the park. Opposite the window and on either side of the fireplace the walls were lined with bookcases filled with books and stacked up to the ceiling with newspapers and manuscripts. Opposite the fireplace on one side of the window were two tables piled up with papers, books and newspapers; in the middle of the room, well in the light, stood a small, plain desk (three foot by two) and a wooden armchair; between the armchair and the bookcase, opposite the window, was a leather sofa on which Marx used to lie down for a rest from time to time. On the mantelpiece were more books, cigars, matches, tobacco boxes, paperweights and photographs of Marx's daughters and wife, Wilhelm Wolff[1] and Frederick Engels.

Marx was a heavy smoker. "*Capital*," he said to me once, "will not even pay for the cigars I smoked writing it." But he was still heavier on matches. He so often forgot his pipe or cigar that he emptied an incredible number of boxes of matches in a short time to relight them.

He never allowed anybody to put his books or papers in order—or rather in disorder. The disorder in which they lay was only apparent, everything was really in its intended place so that it was easy for him to lay his hand on the book or notebook he needed. Even during conversations he often paused to show in the book a quotation or figure he had just mentioned. He and his study were one: the books and papers in it were as much under his control as his own limbs.

Marx had no use for formal symmetry in the arrangement of his books: volumes of different sizes and pamphlets stood next to one another. He arranged them according to their contents, not their size. Books were tools for his mind, not articles of luxury. "They are my slaves and they must serve me as I will," he used to say. He paid no heed to size or binding, quality of paper or type; he would turn down the corners of the pages, make pencil marks in the margin and underline whole lines. He never wrote on books, but sometimes he could not refrain from an exclamation or question mark when the author went too far. His system of underlining made it easy for him to find any passage he

---

[1] *Wolff, Wilhelm* (1809-1864)—German proletarian revolutionary, friend and associate of Marx and Engels, to whom Marx dedicated his *Capital*.—*Ed.*

needed in any book. He had the habit of going through his notebooks and reading the passages underlined in the books after intervals of many years in order to keep them fresh in his memory. He had an extraordinarily reliable memory which he had cultivated from his youth according to Hegel's advice by learning by heart verse in a foreign language he did not know.

He knew Heine and Goethe by heart and often quoted them in his conversations; he was an assiduous reader of poets in all European languages. Every year he read Aeschylus[1] in the Greek original. He considered him and Shakespeare as the greatest dramatic geniuses humanity ever gave birth to. His respect for Shakespeare was boundless: he made a detailed study of his works and knew even the least important of his characters. His whole family had a real cult for the great English dramatist; his three daughters knew many of his works by heart. When after 1848 he wanted to perfect his knowledge of English, which he could already read, he sought out and classified all Shakespeare's original expressions. He did the same with part of the polemical works of William Cobbett,[2] of whom he had a high opinion. Dante and Robert Burns ranked among his favourite poets and he would listen with great pleasure to his daughters reciting or singing the Scottish poet's satires or ballads.

Cuvier, an untirable worker and past master in the sciences, had a suite of rooms, arranged for his personal use, in the Paris Museum, of which he was director. Each room was intended for a particular pursuit and contained the books, instruments, anatomic aids, etc., required for the purpose. When he felt tired of one kind of work he would go into the next room and engage in another; this simple change of mental occupation, it is said, was a rest for him.

Marx was just as tireless a worker as Cuvier, but he had not the means to fit out several studies. He would rest by pacing up and down the room. A strip was worn out from the door to the window, as sharply defined as a track across a meadow.

---

[1] *Aeschylus* (525-456 B.C.)—outstanding Greek dramatist, author of classic tragedies.—*Ed.*

[2] *Cobbett, William* (1762-1835)—English politician and publicist, fought for the democratisation of the British political system.—*Ed.*

From time to time he would lie down on the sofa and read a novel; he sometimes read two or three at a time, alternating one with another. Like Darwin, he was a great reader of novels, his preference being for those of the eighteenth century, particularly Fielding's *Tom Jones*. The more modern novelists whom he found most interesting were Paul de Kock, Charles Lever, Alexander Dumas Senior and Walter Scott, whose *Old Mortality* he considered a masterpiece. He had a definite preference for stories of adventure and humour.

He ranked Cervantes and Balzac above all other novelists. In *Don Quixote* he saw the epic of dying-out chivalry whose virtues were ridiculed and scoffed at in the emerging bourgeois world. He admired Balzac so much that he wished to write a review of his great work *La Comédie Humaine* as soon as he had finished his book on economics. He considered Balzac not only as the historian of his time, but as the prophetic creator of characters which were still in the embryo in the days of Louis Philippe and did not fully develop until after his death, under Napoleon III.

Marx could read all European languages and write in three: German, French and English, to the admiration of language experts. He liked to repeat the saying: "A foreign language is a weapon in the struggle of life."

He had a great talent for languages which his daughters inherited from him. He took up the study of Russian when he was already 50 years old, and although that language had no close affinity to any of the modern or ancient languages he knew, in six months he knew it well enough to derive pleasure from reading Russian poets and prose writers, his preference going to Pushkin, Gogol and Shchedrin. He studied Russian in order to be able to read the documents of official inquiries which were hushed over by the Russian Government because of the political revelations they made. Devoted friends got the documents for Marx and he was certainly the only political economist in Western Europe who had knowledge of them.

Besides the poets and novelists, Marx had another remarkable way of relaxing intellectually—mathematics, for which he had a special liking. Algebra even brought him moral consolation and he took refuge in it in the most distressing moments of his eventful life. During his wife's last illness he was unable to devote himself to his usual scientific work and the only way in which he could shake off the oppression caused by her sufferings was to plunge into mathematics. During that time of moral suffering he wrote a work on infinitesimal calculus which, according to the opinion of experts, is of great scientific value and will be published in his collected works. He saw in higher mathematics the most logical and at the same time the simplest form of dialectical movement. He held the view that a science is not really developed until it has learned to make use of mathematics.

Although Marx's library contained over a thousand volumes carefully collected during his lifelong research work, it was not enough for him, and for years he regularly attended the British Museum, whose catalogue he appreciated very highly.

Even Marx's opponents were forced to acknowledge his extensive and profound erudition, not only in his own speciality—political economy—but in history, philosophy and the literature of all countries.

In spite of the late hour at which Marx went to bed he was always up between eight and nine in the morning, had some black coffee, read through his newspapers and then went to his study, where he worked till two or three in the morning. He interrupted his work only for meals and, when the weather allowed, for a walk on Hampstead Heath in the evening. During the day he sometimes slept for an hour or two on the sofa. In his youth he often worked the whole night through.

Marx had a passion for work. He was so absorbed in it that he often forgot his meals. He had often to be called several times before he came down to the dining-room and hardly had eaten the last mouthful when he was back in his study.

He was a very light eater and even suffered from lack of appetite. This he tried to overcome by highly flavoured food—ham, smoked fish, caviare, pickles. His stomach had to suffer for the enormous activity of his brain. He sacrificed his whole body to his brain; thinking was his greatest enjoyment. I often heard him repeat the words of Hegel, the philosophy master of his youth: "Even the criminal thought of a malefactor has more grandeur and nobility than the wonders of the heavens."

His physical constitution had to be good to put up with this unusual way of life and exhausting mental work. He was, in fact, of powerful build, more than average height, broad-shouldered, deep-chested, and had well-proportioned limbs, although the spinal column was rather long in comparison with the legs, as is often the case with Jews. Had he practised gymnastics in his youth he would have become a very strong man. The only physical exercise he ever pursued regularly was walking: he could ramble or climb hills for hours, chatting and smoking, and not feel at all tired. One can say that he even worked walking in his room, only sitting down for short periods to write what he thought out while walking. He liked to walk up and down while talking, stopping from time to time when the explanation became more animated or the conversation serious.

For many years I went with him on his evening walks on Hampstead Heath and it was while strolling over the meadows with him that I got my education in economics. Without noticing it he expounded to me the whole contents of the first book of *Capital* as he wrote it.

On my return home I always noted as well as I could all I had heard. At first it was difficult for me to follow Marx's profound and complicated reasoning. Unfortunately I have lost those precious notes, for after the Commune the police ransacked and burned my papers in Paris and Bordeaux.

What I regret most is the loss of the notes I took on the evening when Marx, with the abundance of proof and considerations which was typical of him, expounded his brilliant theory of the development of human society. It was as if scales fell from my eyes. For the first time I saw clearly the logic of world history and could trace the apparently so contradictory phenomena of the development of society and ideas to their material origins. I felt dazzled, and the impression remained for years.

The Madrid socialists[1] had the same impression when I developed to them as well as my feeble powers would allow

---

[1] After the defeat of the Paris Commune Lafargue emigrated to Spain, charged by Marx and the General Council of the First International with the fight against the anarchist Bakuninists.—*Ed.*

that most magnificent of Marx's theories, which is beyond doubt one of the greatest ever elaborated by the human brain.

Marx's brain was armed with an unbelievable stock of facts from history and natural science and philosophical theories. He was remarkably skilled in making use of the knowledge and observations accumulated during years of intellectual work. You could question him at any time on any subject and get the most detailed answer you could wish for, always accompanied by philosophical reflexions of general application. His brain was like a man-of-war in port under steam, ready to launch into any sphere of thought.

There is no doubt that *Capital* reveals to us a mind of astonishing vigour and superior knowledge. But for me, as for all those who knew Marx intimately, neither *Capital* nor any other of his works shows all the magnitude of his genius or the extent of his knowledge. He was highly superior to his own works.

I worked with Marx; I was only the scribe to whom he dictated, but that gave me the opportunity of observing his manner of thinking and writing. Work was easy for him, and at the same time difficult. Easy because his mind found no difficulty in embracing the relevant facts and considerations in their completeness. But that very completeness made the exposition of his ideas a matter of long and arduous work....

He saw not only the surface, but what lay beneath it. He examined all the constituent parts in their mutual action and reaction; he isolated each of those parts and traced the history of its development. Then he went on from the thing to its surroundings and observed the reaction of one upon the other. He traced the origin of the object, the changes, evolutions and revolutions it went through, and proceeded finally to its remotest effects. He did not see a thing singly, in itself and for itself, separate from its surroundings: he saw a highly complicated world in continual motion.

His intention was to disclose the whole of that world in its manifold and continually varying action and reaction. Men of letters of Flaubert's and the Goncourts' school complain that it is so difficult to render exactly what one sees; yet all they wish to render is the surface, the impression that they get. Their literary work is child's play in comparison with Marx's: it required extraordinary vigour of thought to grasp reality and render what he saw and wanted to make others see. Marx was never satisfied with his work—he was always making some improvements and he always found his rendering inferior to the idea he wished to convey....

Marx had the two qualities of a genius: he had an incomparable talent for dissecting a thing into its constituent parts, and he was past master at reconstituting the dissected object out of its parts, with all its different forms of development, and discovering their mutual inner relations. His demonstrations were not abstractions—which was the reproach made to him by economists who were themselves incapable of thinking; his method was not that of the geometrician who takes his definitions from the world around him but completely disregards reality in drawing his conclusions. *Capital* does not give isolated definitions or isolated formulas; it gives a series of most searching analyses which bring out the most evasive shades and the most elusive gradations.

Marx begins by stating the plain fact that the wealth of a society dominated by the capitalist mode of production presents itself as an enormous accumulation of commodities; the commodity, which is a concrete object, not a mathematical abstraction, is therefore the element, the cell, of capitalist wealth. Marx now seizes on the commodity, turns it over and over and inside out, and pries out of it one secret after another that official economists were not in the least aware of, although those secrets are more numerous and profound than all the mysteries of the Catholic religion. Having examined the commodity in all its aspects, Marx considers it in its relations to its fellow commodity, in exchange. Then he goes on to its production and the historic prerequisites for its production. He considers the forms which commodities assume and shows how they pass from one to another, how one form is necessarily engendered by the other. He expounds the logical course of development of phenomena with such perfect art that one could think he had imagined it. And yet it is a product of reality, a reproduction of the actual dialectics of the commodity.

Marx was always extremely conscientious about his work: he never gave a fact or figure that was not borne out by the best authorities. He was never satisfied with second-hand information, he always went to the source itself, no matter how tedious the process. To make sure of a minor fact he would go to the British Museum and consult books there. His critics were never able to prove that he was negligent or that he based his arguments on facts which did not bear strict checking.

His habit of always going to the very source made him read authors who were very little known and whom he was the only one to quote. *Capital* contains so many quotations from little-known authors that one might think Marx wanted to show off how well read he was. He had no intention of the sort. "I administer historical justice," he said. "I give each one his due." He considered himself obliged to name the author who had first expressed an idea or formulated it most correctly, no matter how insignificant and little known he was.

Marx was just as conscientious from the literary as from the scientific point of view. Not only would he never base himself on a fact he was not absolutely sure of, he never allowed himself to talk of a thing before he had studied it thoroughly. He did not publish a single work without repeatedly revising it until he had found the most appropriate form. He could not bear to appear in public without thorough preparation. It would have been a torture for him to show his manuscripts before giving them the finishing touch. He felt so strongly about this that he told me one day that he would rather burn his manuscripts than leave them unfinished.

His method of working often imposed upon him tasks the magnitude of which the reader can hardly imagine. Thus, in order to write the twenty pages or so on English factory legislation in *Capital* he went through a whole library of Blue Books containing reports of commissions and factory inspectors in England and Scotland. He read them from cover to cover, as can be seen from the pencil marks in them. He considered those reports as the most important and weighty documents for the study of the capitalist mode of production. He had such a high opinion of those in charge of them that he doubted the possibility of finding in another country in Europe "men as competent, as free from partisanship and respect of persons as are the English factory inspectors". He paid them this brilliant tribute in the Preface to *Capital*.

From these Blue Books Marx drew a wealth of factual information. Many members of Parliament to whom they are distributed use them only as shooting targets, judging the striking power of the gun by the number of pages pierced. Others sell them by the pound, which is the most reasonable thing they can do, for this enabled Marx to buy them cheap from the old paper dealers in Long Acre whom he used to visit to look through their old books and papers. Professor Beesley said that Marx was the man who made the greatest use of English official inquiries and brought them to the knowledge of the world. He did not know that before 1845 Engels took numerous documents from the Blue Books in writing his book on the condition of the working class in England.

2

To get to know and love the heart that beat within the breast of Marx the scholar you had to see him when he had closed his books and notebooks and was surrounded by his family, or again on Sunday evenings in the society of his friends. He then proved the pleasantest of company, full of wit and humour, with a laugh that came straight from the heart. His black eyes under the arches of his bushy brows sparkled with pleasure and malice whenever he heard a witty saying or a pertinent repartee.

He was a loving, gentle and indulgent father. "Children should educate their parents," he used to say. There was never even a trace of the bossy parent in his relations with his daughters, whose love for him was extraordinary. He never gave them an order, but asked them to do what he wished as a favour or made them feel that they should not do what he wanted to forbid them. And yet a father could seldom have had more docile children than he. His daughters considered him as their friend and treated him as a companion; they did not call him "father", but "Moor"—a nickname that he owed to his dark complexion and jet-black hair and beard. The members of the Communist League, on the other hand, called him "Father Marx" before 1848, when he was not even thirty years of age....

Jenny von Westphalen, Marx's wife

Marx, Engels and Marx's daughters in the 1860s

Karl Marx. 1866

Reading room of the British Museum where Marx worked

Trier, birthplace of Karl Marx

London, the Thames

House in Grafton Terrace where Marx lived

Marx used to spend hours playing with his children. These still remember the sea battles in a big basin of water and the burning of the fleets of paper ships that he made for them and set on fire to their great joy.

On Sundays his daughters would not allow him to work, he belonged to them for the whole day. If the weather was fine, the whole family would go for a walk in the country. On their way they would stop at a modest inn for bread and cheese and ginger beer. When his daughters were small he would make the long walk seem shorter to them by telling them endless fantastic tales which he made up as he went, developing and intensifying the complications according to the distance they had to go, so that the little ones forgot their weariness listening.

He had an incomparably fertile imagination: his first literary works were poems. Mrs. Marx carefully preserved the poetry her husband wrote in his youth but never showed it to anybody. His family had dreamt of him being a man of letters or a professor and thought he was debasing himself by engaging in socialist agitation and political economy, which was then disdained in Germany.

Marx had promised his daughters to write a drama on the Gracchi[1] for them. Unfortunately he was unable to keep his word. It would have been interesting to see how he, who was called "the knight of the class struggle", would have dealt with that terrible and magnificent episode in the class struggle of the ancient world. Marx fostered a lot of plans which were never carried out. Among other works he intended to write a Logic and a History of Philosophy, the latter having been his favourite subject in his younger days. He would have needed to live to a hundred to carry out all his literary plans and present the world with a portion of the treasure hidden in his brain.

Marx's wife was his lifelong helpmate in the truest and fullest sense of the word. They had known each other as children and grown up together. Marx was only seventeen at the time of his engagement. Seven long years the young couple had to wait before they were married in 1843. After that they never parted.

---

[1] *Gracchus, Tiberius* (163-133 B.C.) and *Gracchus, Gaius* (153-121 B.C.)—brothers, Roman tribunes; fought for agrarian legislation restricting big landownership.—*Ed.*

Mrs. Marx died shortly before her husband. Nobody ever had a greater sense of equality than she, although she was born and bred in a German aristocratic family. No social differences or classifications existed for her. She entertained working people in their working clothes in her house and at her table with the same politeness and consideration as if they had been dukes or princes. Many workers of all countries enjoyed her hospitality and I am convinced that not one of them ever dreamt that the woman who received them with such homely and sincere cordiality descended in the female line from the family of the Dukes of Argyll and that her brother was a minister of the King of Prussia. That did not worry Mrs. Marx; she had given up everything to follow her Karl and never, not even in times of dire need, was she sorry she had done so.

She had a clear and brilliant mind. Her letters to her friends, written without constraint of effort, are masterly achievements of vigorous and original thinking. It was a treat to get a letter from Mrs. Marx. Johann Philipp Becker[1] published several of her letters. Heine, a pitiless satirist as he was, feared Marx's irony, but he was full of admiration for the penetrating sensitive mind of his wife; when the Marxes were in Paris he was one of their regular visitors.

Marx had such respect for the intelligence and critical sense of his wife that he showed her all his manuscripts and set great store by her opinion, as he himself told me in 1866. Mrs. Marx copied out her husband's manuscripts before they were sent to the print-shop.

Mrs. Marx had a number of children. Three of them died at a tender age during the period of hardships that the family went through after the 1848 Revolution. At that time they lived as emigrants in London in two small rooms in Dean Street, Soho Square. I only knew the three daughters. When I was introduced to Marx in 1865 his youngest daughter, now Mrs. Aveling, was a charming child with a sunny disposition. Marx used to say his wife had made a mistake as to sex when she brought her into the world. The other two daughters formed a most surprising and harmonious

---

[1] *Becker, Johann Philipp* (1809-1886)—German brush-maker; prominent figure in the German and international working-class movement; member of the First International; friend and associate of Marx and Engels.—*Ed.*

contrast. The eldest, Mrs. Longuet, had her father's dark and vigorous complexion, dark eyes and jet-black hair. The second, Mrs. Lafargue, was fair-haired and rosy-skinned, her rich curly hair had a golden shimmer as if it had caught the rays of the setting sun: she was like her mother.

Another important member of the Marx household was Hélène Demuth. Born of a peasant family, she entered the service of Mrs. Marx long before the latter's wedding, when hardly more than a child. When her mistress got married she remained with her and devoted herself with complete self-oblivion to the Marx family. She accompanied her mistress and her husband on all their journeys over Europe and shared their exile. She was the good genius of the house and could always find a way out of the most difficult situations. It was thanks to her sense of order, her economy and skill that the Marx family were at least never short of the bare essentials. There was nothing she could not do: she cooked, kept the house, dressed the children, cut clothes for them and sewed them with Mrs. Marx. She was housekeeper and *major domo* at the same time: she ran the whole house. The children loved her like a mother and her maternal feeling towards them gave her a mother's authority. Mrs. Marx considered her as her bosom friend and Marx fostered a particular friendship towards her; he played chess with her and often enough lost to her.

Hélène loved the Marx family blindly: anything they did was good in her eyes and could not be otherwise; whoever criticised Marx had to deal with her. She extended her motherly protection to everyone who was admitted to intimacy with the Marxes. It was as though she had adopted all of the Marx family. She outlived Marx and his wife and transferred her care to Engels' household. She had known him since she was a girl and extended to him the attachment she had for the Marx family.

Engels was, so to speak, a member of the Marx family. Marx's daughters called him their second father. He was Marx's *alter ego*. For a long time the two names were never separated in Germany and they will be for ever united in history.

Marx and Engels were the personification in our time of the ideal of friendship portrayed by the poets of antiquity. From their youth they developed together and parallel to each other, lived in intimate fellowship of ideas and feelings and shared the same revolutionary agitation; as long as they could live together they worked in common. Had events not parted them for about twenty years they would probably have worked together their whole life. But after the defeat of the 1848 Revolution Engels had to go to Manchester, while Marx was obliged to remain in London. Even so, they continued their common intellectual life by writing to each other almost daily, giving their views on political and scientific events and their work. As soon as Engels was able to free himself from his work he hurried from Manchester to London, where he set up his home only ten minutes away from his dear Marx. From 1870 to the death of his friend not a day went by but the two men saw each other, sometimes at one's house, sometimes at the other's.

It was a day of rejoicing for the Marxes when Engels informed them that he was coming from Manchester. His pending visit was spoken of long beforehand, and on the day of his arrival Marx was so impatient that he could not work. The two friends spent the whole night smoking and drinking together and talking over all that had happened since their last meeting.

Marx appreciated Engels' opinion more than anybody else's, for Engels was the man he considered capable of being his collaborator. For him Engels was a whole audience. No effort could have been too great for Marx to convince Engels and win him over to his ideas. For instance, I have seen him read whole volumes over and over to find the fact he needed to change Engels' opinion on some secondary point that I do not remember concerning the political and religious wars of the Albigenses.[1] It was a triumph for Marx to bring Engels round to his opinion.

Marx was proud of Engels. He took pleasure in enumerating to me all his moral and intellectual qualities. He once specially made the journey to Manchester with me to intro-

---

[1] The *Albigensian wars* were waged from 1209 to 1229 by the feudalists of Northern France and the Pope against the "heretics" of Southern France, the Albigenses, so called after the city of Albi in Southern France. The Albigenses were opposed to sumptuous Catholic rites and the church hierarchy and voiced, in a religious form, the protest of traders and artisans living in southern towns against feudalism.—*Ed*.

duce me to him. He admired the versatility of his knowledge and was alarmed at the slightest thing that could befall him. "I always tremble," he said to me, "for fear he should meet with an accident at the chase. He is so impetuous; he goes galloping over the fields with slackened reins, not shying at any obstacle."

Marx was as good a friend as he was a loving husband and father. In his wife and daughters, Hélène and Engels, he found worthy objects of love for a man such as he was.

3

Having started as leader of the radical bourgeoisie, Marx found himself deserted as soon as his opposition became too resolute and looked upon as an enemy as soon as he became a socialist. He was baited and expelled from Germany after being decried and calumniated, and then there was a conspiracy of silence against him and his work. The *Eighteenth Brumaire*, which proves that Marx was the only historian and politician of 1848 who understood and disclosed the real nature of the causes and results of the *coup d'état* of December 2, 1851,[1] was completely ignored. In spite of the actuality of the work not a single bourgeois newspaper even mentioned it.

The Poverty of Philosophy, an answer to the *Philosophy of Poverty*,[2] and *A Contribution to the Critique of Political Economy* were likewise ignored. The First International and the first book of *Capital* broke this conspiracy of silence after it had lasted fifteen years. Marx could no longer be ignored: the International developed and filled the world with the glory of its achievements. Although Marx kept in the background and let others act it was soon discovered who the man behind the scenes was.

---

[1] *On December 2, 1851*, Louis Bonaparte, nephew of Napoleon I and President of the French Republic, carried out a *coup d'état*, dissolved the Legislative Assembly and proclaimed himself President for life.

On December 2, 1852, he proclaimed himself Emperor Napoleon III.—*Ed.*

[2] *Philosophy of Poverty*—a book by Proudhon, a French petty-bourgeois publicist.—*Ed.*

The Social-Democratic Party was founded in Germany and became a power that Bismarck[1] courted before he attacked it. Schweitzer, a follower of Lassalle,[2] published a series of articles, which Marx highly praised, to bring *Capital* to the knowledge of the working public. On a motion by Johann Philipp Becker the Congress of the International adopted a resolution directing the attention of socialists in all countries to *Capital* as to the "Bible of the working class".[3]

After the rising on March 18, 1871, in which people tried to see the work of the International, and after the defeat of the Commune, which the General Council of the First International took it upon itself to defend against the rage of the bourgeois press in all countries, Marx's name became known to the whole world. He was acknowledged as the greatest theoretician of scientific socialism and the organiser of the first international working-class movement.

Capital became the manual of socialists in all countries. All socialist and working-class papers spread its scientific theories. During a big strike which broke out in New York extracts from *Capital* were published in the form of leaflets to inspire the workers to endurance and show them how justified their claims were.

Capital was translated into the main European languages —Russian, French and English, and extracts were published in German, Italian, French, Spanish and Dutch. Every time attempts were made by opponents in Europe or America to refute its theories, the economists immediately got a socialist reply which closed their mouths. *Capital* is really today what it was called by the Congress of the International— *the Bible of the working class.*

The share Marx had to take in the international socialist movement took time from his scientific activity. The death

---

[1] *Bismarck, Otto* (1815-1898)—Prussian statesman, Chancellor of the German Empire from 1871.—*Ed.*

[2] *Lassalle, Ferdinand* (1825-1864)—German petty-bourgeois socialist, founder of the General Association of German Workers (1863). Marx and Engels sharply criticised the theory, tactics and organisational principles of Lassalleanism as an opportunist trend in the German working-class movement.—*Ed.*

[3] This resolution was adopted by the Brussels Congress of the First International in September 1868.—*Ed.*

of his wife and that of his eldest daughter, Mrs. Longuet, also had an adverse effect upon it.

Marx's love for his wife was profound and intimate. Her beauty had been his pride and his joy, her gentleness and devotedness had lightened for him the hardships necessarily resulting from his eventful life as a revolutionary socialist. The disease which led to the death of Jenny Marx also shortened the life of her husband. During her long and painful illness Marx, exhausted by sleeplessness and lack of exercise and fresh air and morally weary, contracted the pneumonia which was to snatch him away.

On December 2, 1881, Mrs. Marx died as she had lived, a Communist and a materialist. Death had no terrors for her. When she felt her end approach she exclaimed: "Karl, my strength is ebbing." Those were her last intelligible words.

She was buried in Highgate Cemetery, in unconsecrated ground, on December 5. Conforming to the habits of her life and Marx's, all care was taken to avoid her funeral being made a public one and only a few close friends accompanied her to her last resting-place. Marx's old friend Engels delivered the address over her grave....

After the death of his wife, Marx's life was a succession of physical and moral sufferings which he bore with great fortitude. They were aggravated by the sudden death of his eldest daughter, Mrs. Longuet, a year later. He was broken, never to recover.

He died at his desk on March 14, 1883, at the age of sixty-four.

Paul Lafargue

REMINISCENCES OF ENGELS[1]

I made Engels' acquaintance in 1867, the year the first volume of *Capital* appeared.

"Now that you are my daughter's fiancé I must introduce you to Engels," Marx said to me, and we set out for Manchester.

Engels lived with his wife and her niece, then six or seven years old, in a little house on the outskirts of the town. A few steps farther and you were in the fields....

Like Marx Engels had emigrated to London after the defeat of the revolution on the continent and like him he wanted to devote himself to political agitation and scientific study.

But Marx had lost his and his wife's means in the storm of revolution and Engels had nothing to live on either. Engels therefore had to accept his father's invitation and return to Manchester. There he resumed the clerical job in his father's business that he had had in 1843, while Marx was hardly able to provide for the most pressing necessities of his family by weekly contributions to the *New York Daily Tribune*.

Engels led a sort of double life from then until 1870: on weekdays from 10 to 4 he was a business man whose main occupation was to deal with the firm's correspondence in several languages and to attend the Exchange. He had an official residence in the centre of the town where he

---

[1] Published in 1905.—*Ed.*

Frederick Engels. 1839

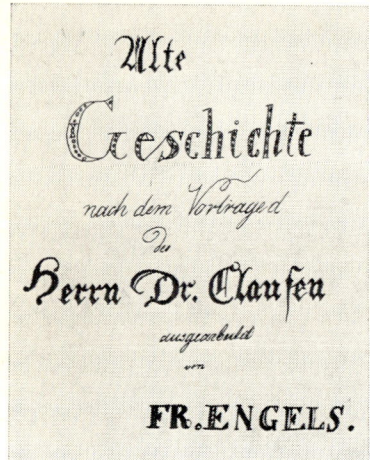
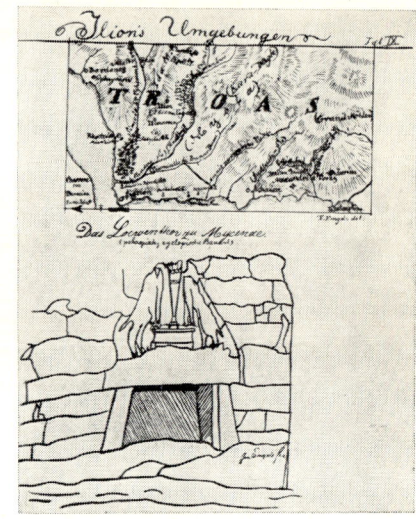
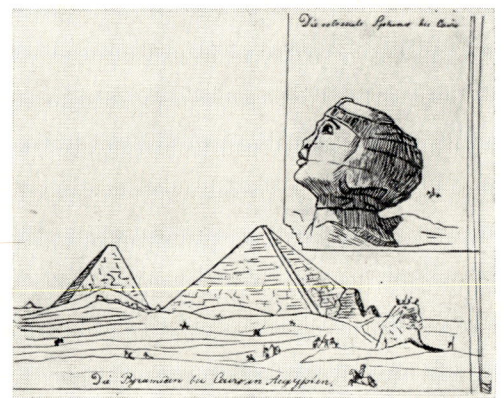

Notes on ancient history in Engels' exercise-book

Frederick Engels. 1840s

A view of Brussels

entertained his business friends, but it was in his little house on the outskirts that he received his political and scientific friends, including the chemist Schorlemmer and Samuel Moore, who later translated the first volume of *Capital* into English.

His wife, who was of Irish descent and an ardent patriot, was in continual touch with the many Irishmen in Manchester and was always well informed of their conspiracies. More than one Sinn Feiner[1] found hospitality in Engels' house and it was thanks to his wife that the leader in the attempt to free the condemned Sinn Feiners on their way to the scaffold was able to evade the police. Engels, who took an interest in the Sinn Fein movement, collected documents for a history of the English domination in Ireland: he must have written parts of it and they should be among his papers.

In the evening, after the slavery of business, he would go home, a free man again. He took part not only in the business life of the Manchester manufacturers, but in their pleasures as well, attending their meetings, their dinners and their sports events. He was an excellent rider and had his own hunter for the fox chase; when the neighbouring gentry and aristocracy sent out invitations to all riders in the district according to the ancient feudal custom he never failed to attend. He was always among the leaders in clearing ditches, hedges and other obstacles. "I always fear that some day I shall hear he has had an accident," Marx once said to me....

I do not know whether his bourgeois acquaintances were aware of his other life: the English are so extraordinarily discreet and show so little curiosity about what does not concern them. In any case, they knew nothing about the high intellectual qualities of the man with whom they had daily intercourse, for Engels showed them little of his knowledge. He whom Marx esteemed as the most learned man in Europe was nothing to them but a merry companion who could appreciate a glass of good wine....

Engels never lost his love for the society of the young and he was always an admirable host. Many were the Lon-

---

[1] *Sinn Feiners*—Irish petty-bourgeois revolutionaries of the 1850s-1870s who fought for the national independence of Ireland.—*Ed.*

don socialists, the comrades passing through and the emigrants from all countries who gathered at his hospitable table on Sundays. They all left his house delighted with those evenings of which he was the soul with his gaiety, his wit and his never-failing cheerfulness.

* * *

One cannot think of Engels without immediately remembering Marx, and *vice versa*; their lives interwove so closely that they seemed to form one single life. Yet they both had very distinct individualities and differed from each other not only outwardly but in temperament, character and way of thinking and feeling.

They made each other's acquaintance towards the end of November 1842 when Engels called at the editorial office of the *Rheinische Zeitung*. After the suspension of the *Rheinische Zeitung* by the censor, Marx got married and went to France. Engels paid him a few days' visit in Paris in September 1844. Since their joint work for the *Deutsch-Französische Jahrbücher*, Engels informs us in his biography of Marx, they kept up correspondence with each other and it was from that time that a collaboration dated which ended only with the death of Marx. At the beginning of 1845 Marx was expelled from France by Guizot's ministry on the demand of the Prussian Government and went to Brussels; shortly afterwards Engels also went there, and when the 1848 Revolution again brought the *Rheinische Zeitung*[1] to life Engels was at Marx's side and managed the newspaper in his place when he was obliged to absent himself.

In spite of his intellectual superiority Engels never won the same authority as Marx over his colleagues on the editorial board—young men distinguished by their talent, their revolutionary spirit and their courage in the struggle. Marx told me that on his return from a journey to Vienna he found the editorial board split by quarrels that Engels had not been able to settle; antagonisms were so sharp that it seemed they could be settled only by a duel. Marx needed all his diplomacy to restore peace.

Marx was a born leader; he influenced everybody who

---

[1] Here the *Neue Rheinische Zeitung* is meant. It appeared in Cologne in 1848-49, with Marx as its editor-in-chief.—*Ed.*

came in contact with him. Engels was the first to admit this; he often told me that Marx had impressed everybody since his youth by the clearness and resoluteness of his character and that he was a real leader enjoying the full confidence of all even in matters which lay outside his sphere, as the following fact proves.

Wolff, to whom the first book of *Capital* is dedicated, fell seriously ill at his home in Manchester. The physicians had given up all hope, but Engels and his friends would not believe the terrible sentence and unanimously decided that Marx must be wired to come and give his opinion....

Engels and Marx had the habit of working together; although Engels carried exactitude to the extreme, he sometimes became impatient at the scrupulousness of Marx, who would not put a sentence on paper unless he could prove it in a dozen different ways.

After the defeat of the 1848 Revolution the two friends had to part. One went to Manchester, the other remained in London. But they did not cease to live together in thought and every day, or almost, for twenty years they informed each other by letter of their impressions and considerations on political events and their progress in their studies. Their correspondence has been preserved to this day.

Engels left Manchester as soon as he was able to free himself from the burden of business life; he hurried to London and took up his residence at Regent's Park Road, ten minutes from Maitland Park, where Marx lived. Every day at about one he went to see Marx, and when the weather was fine and Marx was so disposed they went for a walk together on Hampstead Heath; if not, they chatted for an hour or two, walking up and down in Marx's study, one diagonally in one way, the other in the other.

I remember a discussion on the Albigenses that lasted for several days. At the time Marx was studying the role of Jewish and Christian financiers in the Middle Ages. In the intervals between their meetings they studied the disputed question in order to form a common opinion. No other criticism of their thoughts and work was as valuable for them as their mutual criticism. They had the highest opinion of each other.

Marx never tired of admiring the universality of Engels' knowledge and the wonderful versatility of his mind which allowed him to pass with ease from one subject to another, while Engels took pleasure in admitting the force of Marx's analysis and synthesis.

"Naturally," Engels said to me one day, "the understanding and exposition of the mechanism of the capitalist mode of production would have been achieved in any case and the laws of its development would have been disclosed and explained; but it would have taken a long time and it would have been piece and patch work. Marx alone was capable of following all the economic categories in their dialectic motion, to link the phases of their development with the causes determining it, and to reconstruct the edifice of the whole of economics in a monument of science the individual parts of which mutually supported and determined one another."

It was not only their brains that worked in unison, they had the warmest friendship for each other: one always thought what could please the other, one was proud of the other. One day Marx got a letter from his Hamburg publisher telling him of a visit he had had from Engels, whom he had come to consider as one of the most charming men he had ever met. "I should like to see the man," Marx called out as he read the letter, "who does not find Fred just as amiable as he is learned!"

Money, knowledge—everything was in common between them. When Marx became a correspondent of the *New York Daily Tribune* he was still learning English: Engels translated his articles and even wrote them when necessary. And when Engels was preparing his *Anti-Dühring* Marx interrupted the work he was doing to write an essay on economics of which Engels used a part, as he publicly stated.

Engels extended his friendship to the whole of Marx's family: Marx's daughters were as children to him, they called him their second father. This friendship lasted beyond the grave.

After Marx's death Engels was the only one who could go through his manuscripts and publish the works he left behind. He laid aside his general philosophy of science, on which he had been working for more than ten years and for which he had made a review of all sciences and their progress up to date, in order to devote himself entirely to the last two books of *Capital*.

Engels loved study for its own sake: he was interested in all fields. In 1849, after the defeat of the revolution, he went to England from Genoa on a sailing vessel, for he thought it risky to go from Switzerland via France. He profited by this opportunity to study nautical questions: during the trip he kept a diary in which he recorded the changes in the position of the sun, the direction of the wind, the state of the sea, etc. This diary must be among his papers, for the restless and impetuous Engels was as methodical as an old maid. He kept everything and registered it with the most scrupulous exactitude.

Philology and military science had been his first favourites: he never gave them up and always kept abreast of their progress. He considered the tiniest details important. I remember how in order to learn stress in Spanish, he read *Romancero* aloud with his friend Mesa who had come from Spain.

His knowledge of European languages and even dialects was unbelievable.

When, after the fall of the Commune, I met the members of the National Council of the International in Spain, they told me that somebody called "Angel" was replacing me as secretary of the General Council for Spain and that he wrote perfect Castilian. "Angel" was Engels with his name pronounced in the Spanish way. When I went to Lisbon, Francia, secretary of the National Council for Portugal, told me he had got letters from Engels in impeccable Portuguese—a fine achievement when one thinks of the similarities and small differences the two languages have with one another and with Italian, in which he was equally proficient.

Engels made it a point of vanity to write to his correspondents in their mother tongue: he wrote to Lavrov[1] in Russian, to Frenchmen in French, to Poles in Polish, and so on. He enjoyed reading in local dialects and lost no time in ordering Bignami's[2] popular works in the Milan dialect.

One of the sights on Ramsgate Beach that was much

---

[1] *Lavrov, Pyotr Lavrovich* (1823-1900)—Russian publicist, Narodnik, member of the First International, participant in the Paris Commune.—*Ed.*

[2] *Bignami, Enrico* (1846-1921)—participant in the Italian national liberation movement, publicist and publisher.—*Ed.*

enjoyed by common Londoners was a bearded dwarf in a Brazilian general's uniform. Engels spoke to him in Portuguese and then in Spanish but got no answer. At last the general said a word or two. "Why, your Brazilian is an Irishman!" Engels exclaimed, and he hailed him in his native dialect. The poor fellow wept for joy.

"Engels stutters in twenty languages," said a Commune emigrant, joking at the way Engels stuttered when he was excited.

No field left Engels indifferent; in the last years of his life he began to read works on childbirth because Mrs. Freyberger,[1] who lived in his house, was preparing for an examination in medicine.

Marx reproached him for scattering his attention over so many subjects just for pleasure "without thinking of working for humanity". Engels retorted: "It would be a pleasure for me to burn the Russian publications on agriculture that have been preventing you for years from finishing *Capital*."

At that time Marx had taken up the study of Russian because Danielson, one of his Petersburg friends, had sent him numerous bulky reports on agricultural investigations the publication of which was forbidden by the Russian Government because of the terrible situation they revealed.

Engels' impulse for knowledge was not satisfied until he had mastered his subject in the smallest details. Anybody who has an idea of the extent and variety of his knowledge and at the same time considers his active life is astonished that Engels, who had nothing of the armchair scientist about him, could manage to store such an amount of knowledge in his head. With a memory which was as sure as all-embracing and an extraordinary speed at work he combined a no less remarkable ease of understanding.

He worked quickly and without effort. In his large, well-lighted studies, whose walls were lined with bookcases, there was not a scrap of paper on the floor, and all his books were in their places with the exception of a dozen or so on his desk. The rooms were more like reception-rooms than a scholar's study.

---

[1] *Freyberger (Kautsky), Louise*—Austrian socialist, Engels' secretary from 1890.—*Ed.*

He was just as particular about his appearance: he was always trim and scrupulously clean, always looking as though ready to go to a parade as during his year's voluntary service in the Prussian army. I do not know anybody who wore the same clothes for such a long time without creasing them or making them shabby. He was economical as far as his personal needs were concerned and incurred only such expenses as he deemed absolutely necessary, but his generosity towards the Party and his Party comrades when they applied to him in need knew no bounds.

* * *

Engels was living in Manchester when the First International was founded.... He supported the International financially and contributed to its paper *The Commonwealth*, founded by the General Council. After the declaration of the Franco-Prussian war and his move to London[1] he devoted himself to its development with the zeal that he displayed in everything that he undertook.

At first it was military tactics that interested him in the war: he followed the opposing armies day by day and more than once foretold the steps the German General Staff would take, as is proved by his articles in *Pall Mall Gazette*.[2] He foretold the surrounding of Napoleon's army two days before Sedan.[3] These prophecies, which, by the way, were greatly commented on in the English press, made Marx's eldest daughter Jenny give him the title of "General". After the fall of the French Empire he had but one wish and one hope: the triumph of the French Republic. Engels and Marx had no fatherland: they were both, to use Marx's expression, citizens of the world.

---

[1] In September 1870.—*Ed*.

[2] A paper published in London from 1865. Engels' articles on the Franco-Prussian war appeared in it from July 1870 to March 1871.—*Ed*.

[3] During the battle at Sedan on September 1, 1870, the French army, together with Napoleon III, was surrounded and on September 2 it capitulated.—*Ed*.

Wilhelm Liebknecht

REMINISCENCES OF MARX[1]

Hundreds of times I have been urged to write about Marx and my personal association with him, and every time I have refused. It was out of respect for Marx that I did so. For perhaps the task was beyond me or I would not have the time. And it would be insulting to Marx's memory to write about him in a hasty, slipshod way.

But it was objected that a cursory sketch need not necessarily be slipshod or hasty, that I could tell things which nobody else could and that anything which can help our workers or our Party to know Marx better is of incontestable value. And if the choice is between a relation, imperfect as it must be, of what I know, or nothing at all, the former is certainly the lesser evil. In the end I had to agree....

Marx, the man of science, the editor of the *Rheinische Zeitung*, the co-founder of the *Deutsch-Französische Jahrbücher*, the co-author of the *Communist Manifesto*, the editor of the *Neue Rheinische Zeitung* and the creator of *Capital*, is a figure belonging to the public.... It would be foolhardy of me to try to write about that Marx, for I could not do so in the short time that I could snatch from my urgent daily work. That would require profound scientific work. Where could I get the time from?...

---

[1] *Liebknecht, Wilhelm* (1826-1900)—prominent figure in the German and international working-class movement, one of the founders and leaders of German Social-Democracy; friend and associate of Marx and Engels.

These reminiscences were published in 1896.—*Ed.*

I shall therefore refer to Marx, the man of science and of politics, only incidentally and biographically in this short sketch. That aspect of Marx is clear to everybody. I shall try to show the *man* in Marx, as I knew him myself.

1
First Meeting with Marx

My friendship with Marx's two eldest daughters—they were then six and seven years old respectively—began a few days after I arrived in London after being released from prison in "Free Switzerland" and travelling via France on a compulsory passport. I met the Marx family at the summer fête of the Communist Workers' Educational Society[1] somewhere near London, I do not remember whether it was at Greenwich or Hampton Court.

"Père Marx", whom I had never seen before, at once severely scrutinised me, looking searchingly into my eyes and attentively surveying my head....

The scrutiny ended favourably and I endured the gaze of that lion-like head with the jet-black mane. Then came a lively, cheerful chat and we were soon in the middle of unconstrained rejoicing, Marx being the least constrained of all. I was immediately introduced to Mrs. Marx, Lenchen, who had been their faithful housekeeper since she was a girl, and the children. From that day I was at home in Marx's house and not a day went by but I visited his family. They were living in Dean Street, off Oxford Street. I took up lodgings in Church Street, not far away.

2
First Conversation

I had my first long talk with Marx the day after I met him at the fête which I have just mentioned. We had naturally not been able to have a serious discussion there and Marx invited me for the next day to the premises of

[1] *The German Workers' Educational Society* was founded in London in 1840. Marx had a decisive influence in it in 1847-50 and in the sixties and seventies.—*Ed.*

the Workers' Educational Society, where Engels would probably be too.

I arrived somewhat before the appointed time. Marx had not yet arrived, but I met a number of old acquaintances and was in the middle of an animated conversation when Marx slapped me on the shoulder with a friendly greeting, telling me that Engels was downstairs in the private parlour and that we would be more to ourselves there.

I did not know what a private parlour was and I thought that the time for the big test had come, but I went trustingly with Marx. The impression he made on me was just as favourable as the day before—he had a gift for inspiring confidence. He slipped his arm through mine and took me to the private parlour where Engels, who was already sitting there with a pewter mug of dark stout, gave me a cheerful welcome.

Amy, the brisk barmaid, was immediately ordered to bring us something to drink—and to eat too, for food was one of the major questions for us emigrants—and we sat down, I on one side of the table, Marx and Engels on the other. The heavy mahogany table, the shining tankards, the frothing stout, the prospect of a real English beefsteak and all that goes with it, and the long clay pipes only asking to be smoked made one feel so comfortable that it reminded me of one of the English illustrations to *Boz*. But it was to be an examination after all! Well, I would manage it alright. The conversation got livelier....

I had never had any personal association with Marx or Engels before I met Engels in Geneva the year before. The only works by them that I knew were Marx's articles in the Paris *Jahrbücher*[1] and *The Poverty of Philosophy* and Engels' *Condition of the Working Class in England*. A Communist since 1846, I had only been able to procure the *Communist Manifesto* a short time before I met Engels after the Reich Constitution campaign,[2] although I had, of course, heard of it earlier and knew its contents. As for the *Neue Rheinische Zeitung*, I had seldom been able to see it, for during the eleven months it appeared I was either

---

[1] *Deutsch-Französische Jahrbücher.—Ed.*
[2] Revolutionary struggle in South-West Germany in the spring and summer of 1849 for an All-German (Reich) Constitution.—*Ed.*

abroad, in prison, or living the chaotic and stormy life of a rebel volunteer.

Both my examiners suspected me of petty-bourgeois "democracy" and "South-German placidity", and some of the opinions I expressed on men and things met severe criticism.... But on the whole the examination was not a failure and the conversation turned to broader questions.

Soon we were talking about natural sciences and Marx scoffed at the victorious reaction in Europe who imagined that they had stifled the revolution and had no idea that natural science was preparing a new one. King Steam, who had revolutionised the world the century before, had lost his throne and was being superseded by a still greater revolutionary—the electric spark. Then Marx told me with great enthusiasm about the model of an electric engine that had been on show for a few days in Regent Street and that could drive a railway train.

"The problem is now solved," he said, "and the consequences are unpredictable. The economic revolution must necessarily be followed by a political revolution, for the latter is but the expression of the former."

The way Marx spoke of the progress of science and mechanics showed so clearly his world outlook, especially what was later to be called the materialist conception of history, that certain doubts which I still entertained melted like snow in the spring sun.

I did not return home that evening. We talked, laughed and drank until well into the morning and the sun was already up when I went to bed. But I did not stay there long; I could not get to sleep, for my mind was full of all I had heard and the tumult of my thoughts drove me out of bed and to Regent Street to see the model, the modern horse of Troy which bourgeois society in its suicidal blindness had brought into its Ilion amidst rejoicings like the Trojans of old and which was to be their inevitable ruin. *Essetai haemar*—the day will come when holy Ilion will fall.

A big crowd showed me where the engine was exhibited. I pushed my way through and there was the engine and the train racing round merrily....

That was in 1850, at the beginning of July.

3
Marx, Teacher and Educator of Revolutionaries

"Moor", being five or six years older than us "young fellows", was conscious of the advantage his maturity gave him over us and sounded us, particularly me, on every possible occasion. Well-read as he was and with his fabulous memory, he had no difficulty in making it hot for us. How he enjoyed it when he could give one of the "student boys" a sticky question and prove at his expense in *corpore vili* the wretchedness of our universities and academic education.

But he educated us and there was a plan in his education. I can say that he was my teacher in both senses of the word, the stricter and the broader. We had to learn from him in all branches, not to mention political economy—you don't talk of the pope in his palace. I shall speak of his talks on that subject in the Communist League later. Marx was at his ease in ancient as well as modern languages. I was a philologist and it gave him childlike pleasure when he could show me some difficult passage from Aristotle[1] or Aeschylus which I could not immediately construe correctly. How he scolded me one day because I did not know... Spanish! He snatched up *Don Quixote* out of a pile of books and began to give me a lesson. I already knew the principles of grammar and word building from Diez's comparative grammar of the Romance languages and so I got on pretty well under his excellent direction and with his cautious help when I hesitated or got stuck. And what a patient teacher he was, he who was otherwise so fiery! The lesson was cut short only by the entrance of a visitor. Every day I was questioned and had to translate a passage from *Don Quixote* or some other Spanish book until he judged me capable enough.

Marx was a remarkable philologist, though more in modern than in ancient languages. He had a most exact knowledge of Grimm's German Grammar and he understood more about the part of the Grimm brothers' dictionary that was published than I, a linguist. He could write English

---

[1] *Aristotle* (384-322 B.C.)—outstanding Greek philosopher and scientist.—*Ed.*

and French as well as an Englishman or Frenchman, though his pronunciation was faulty. His articles for the *New York Daily Tribune* were written in classical English, his *Poverty of Philosophy* against Proudhon's *Philosophy of Poverty* in classical French. The French friend to whom he showed the manuscript of the latter work before it was printed found but little to improve in it.

As Marx understood the essence of language and had studied its origin, its development and its structure, it was not difficult for him to learn languages. In London he learned Russian and during the Crimean War he even intended to study Turkish and Arabic, but he was not able to do so. As one who really wishes to master a language, he attached most importance to reading. A man with a good memory—and Marx's was of such extraordinary fidelity that it never forgot anything—quickly accumulates vocabulary and turns of phrases. Practical use is then easily learned.

In 1850 and 1851 Marx gave a course of lectures on political economy. He was reluctant to do so, but once he had given a few private lectures to some of his closest friends he let us persuade him to lecture to broader audiences. In this course, which was thoroughly enjoyed by all fortunate to attend, Marx fully developed the principles of his system as we see it expounded in *Capital*. In the overcrowded hall of the Communist Educational Society, which at the time was in Great Windmill Street,—the very hall in which the *Communist Manifesto* had been adopted a year and a half before—Marx showed a great gift for popularising knowledge. Nobody was more against vulgarising science, i.e., falsifying, debasing and stultifying it, than he was. Nobody had a greater talent for expressing himself clearly. Clarity of speech is the fruit of clarity of thought: clear thought necessarily leads to clear expression.

Marx proceeded with method. He formulated a proposition—as briefly as possible—and then explained it at length, avoiding with the utmost care any expressions which the workers would not understand. Then he invited his listeners to ask questions. If none were asked he would begin examining, which he did with such pedagogical skill that no gap or misunderstanding escaped him.

Expressing my surprise at this skill one day, I was told that Marx had already given lectures in the Workers'

Society in Brussels.¹ In any case, he had all that makes an excellent teacher. In teaching he also made use of a blackboard on which he wrote formulas, including those that we all know from the beginning of *Capital*.

The pity was that the course only lasted about six months or less. Elements which Marx did not like got into the Communist Educational Society. When the tide of emigration had ebbed the Society shrivelled up and became somewhat sectarian, the old followers of Weitling² and Cabet³ began to assert themselves again. Marx, who was not content with such a narrow scope of activity and could do more important things than sweep away old cobwebs, kept away from the Society.

Marx was a purist in language to the extent of pedanticism. My Upper Hessian dialect, which clung to me like a skin—or perhaps I clung to it—let me in for countless lectures from him. If I speak of such trifles it is only because they show how much Marx felt himself to be the teacher of us "young fellows".

This was naturally manifested in another way. He was very exacting towards us. As soon as he discovered a deficiency in our knowledge he would insist most forcibly on our making it up and give us the right advice how to do so. Anybody who was alone with him would be put through a regular examination. Such examinations were no joke. You could not throw dust in his eyes. If he saw that his efforts were lost on anybody that was the end of his friendship. It was an honour for us to be "school-mastered" by him. I was never with him but I learned something from him....

In those days only a small minority in the working class itself had risen to the level of socialism, and among the socialists themselves only a minority were socialists in the scientific sense Marx gave the word—the sense of the *Communist Manifesto*. The bulk of the workers, if they

---

[1] The German Workers' Educational Society in Brussels was founded by Marx and Engels in August 1847 with a view to giving political education to the masses and disseminating ideas of scientific communism. It ceased to exist soon after the February bourgeois revolution of 1848 in France.—*Ed*.

[2] *Weitling, Wilhelm* (1808-1871)—one of the theoreticians of equalitarian utopian communism; tailor by trade.—*Ed*.

[3] *Cabet, Etienne* (1788-1856)—prominent representative of utopian communism, founder of a communistic colony in America.—*Ed*.

were at all awakened to political life, were pinned down by the mist of sentimental democratic wishes and phrases, such as were characteristic of the 1848 movement and what preceded and followed it. The applause of the multitude, popularity, was for Marx a proof that one was on the wrong road, and his favourite motto was Dante's proud line: *Segui il tuo corso, e lascia dir le genti!*—Go your own way and let tongues wag!

How often he quoted that line, with which he also concluded his Preface to *Capital*. Nobody is insensitive to blows, jostling, or gnat or bug bites, and how often Marx, attacked from all sides and racked by the struggle for existence, misunderstood by the working people the weapons for whose emancipation he forged in the silence of the night, sometimes even disdained by them whereas they followed vain prattlers, dissembling traitors or even avowed enemies —how often he must have repeated to himself in the solitude of his poor, genuinely proletarian study the words of the great Florentine to inspire himself with courage and fresh energy!

He would not be led astray. Unlike the prince in the *Thousand and One Nights* who surrendered victory and the prize of victory because, terrified by the noise and the fearful apparitions round him, he looked round and back, Marx went forward, always looking ahead at his bright goal....

As great as his hatred for popularity was his anger at those who sought it. He loathed fine speakers and woe betide anyone who engaged in phrasemongering. With such people he was implacable. "Phrasemonger" was the worst reproach he could make, and when he had once discovered that somebody was a phrasemonger it was all over with him. He kept impressing upon us "young fellows" the necessity for logical thought and clarity in expression and forced us to study.

The magnificent reading-room of the British Museum with its inexhaustible treasure of books was completed about that time. Marx went there daily and urged us to go too. Study! Study! That was the categoric injunction that we heard often enough from him and that he gave us by his example and the continual work of his mighty brain.

While the other emigrants were daily planning a world

revolution and day after day, night after night, intoxicating themselves with the opium-like motto: "Tomorrow it will begin!", we, the "brimstone band", the "bandits", the "dregs of mankind", spent our time in the British Museum and tried to educate ourselves and prepare arms and ammunition for the future fight.

Sometimes we had not a bite to eat, but that did not keep us away from the Museum, for there we had comfortable chairs to sit on and in winter it was warm and cosy, which was far from being the case at home, for those who had a home.

Marx was a stern teacher: he not only urged us to study, he made sure that we did so.

For a long time I was studying the history of the English trade unions. Every day he would ask me how far I had got and he left me no peace until I delivered a long speech to a large audience. He was present at it. He did not praise me, but neither did he inflict any devastating criticism, and as he was not in the habit of praising and did so only out of pity, I consoled myself for the absence of praise. Then, when he entered into a discussion with me over an assertion that I had made, I considered that as indirect praise.

As a teacher Marx had the rare quality of being severe without discouraging. And another of his remarkable qualities was that he compelled us to be critical of ourselves and would not allow us to be complacent over our achievements. He scourged bland contemplativeness cruelly with the lash of his irony.

4

Marx's Style

If Buffon's[1] saying: "The style is the man" is true of anybody, it is of Marx—Marx's style is Marx. A man of such thorough truthfulness as Marx, who knew no other cult but that of the truth, who swept aside in a moment a proposition painfully arrived at, and therefore dear to him, as soon as he was convinced of its incorrectness, necessarily

---

[1] *Buffon, George Louis* (1707-1788)—outstanding French naturalist. —*Ed.*

showed himself in his works as he was in reality. Incapable of hypocrisy, dissimulation or pretence, he was always himself, in his writings as in his life. Naturally, the style of such a many-sided, versatile and all-embracing nature as his could not have the uniformity, evenness or even monotony of a less complex, less comprehensive one. The Marx of *Capital,* the Marx of *The Eighteenth Brumaire* and the Marx of *Herr Vogt* are three different Marxes; yet in their variety they are *one* Marx, there is unity in their trinity, the unity of his great personality which manifests itself in different ways in different fields and yet is ever the selfsame.

The style of *Capital* is admittedly difficult to understand, but then, is the subject treated easy to understand? Style is not only the man, it is also the material, it must be adapted to the material. There is no royal road to science, each one must strain himself and climb, even if he has the best of leaders. To complain of the difficult, abstruse or even heavy style of *Capital* is only to admit one's own mental laziness or inability to think.

Is *The Eighteenth Brumaire* unintelligible? Is an arrow unintelligible that flies straight to the target and penetrates deep into it? Is a javelin unintelligible which, aimed by a steady hand, pierces the very centre of the enemy's heart? The words of *The Eighteenth Brumaire* are arrows and javelins, they are a style that brands and kills. If ever hate, scorn and burning love of liberty were expressed in burning, devastating, lofty words, it is in *The Eighteenth Brumaire,* which combines the indignant severity of a Tacitus[1] with the deadly satire of a Juvenal[2] and the holy wrath of a Dante. Style here is the *stilus* that it was of old in the hand of the Romans, a sharp stiletto, used to write and to stab. Style is a dagger which strikes unerringly at the heart.

And in *Herr Vogt,* what sparkling wit, what Shakespeare-like gaiety at finding a Falstaff[3] and in him an inexhaustible mine to fill an arsenal of irony!

Marx's style is indeed Marx himself. He has been

---

[1] *Tacitus* (c. 55-c. 120 A.D.)—famous Roman historian.—*Ed.*
[2] *Juvenal* (born about mid-1st cent., died after 127)—famous Roman satirical poet.—*Ed.*
[3] *Falstaff*—personage from Shakespeare's *Henry IV* and *Merry Wives of Windsor.—Ed.*

reproached with trying to squeeze as much content as possible into the minimum space, but that is precisely Marx.

Marx attached extreme importance to purity and correctness of expression. And he chose himself the highest masters in Goethe, Lessing, Shakespeare, Dante and Cervantes, from whom he made almost daily readings. He was most scrupulous as far as purity and correctness of language were concerned. I remember that he once gave me a lecture at the beginning of my stay in London for having used the expression *"stattgehabte Versammlung"* in an article. I pleaded usage as an excuse but Marx burst out: "What wretched German Gymnasiums where no German is taught! What wretched German universities!" and so on. I defended myself as best I could and quoted examples from the classics, but I never spoke of a *"stattgehabte"* or *"stattgefundene"* event again and tried to get others out of the habit....

Marx was a strict purist, he often searched hard and long for the correct expression. He hated unnecessary foreign words and if he did frequently use foreign words where the subject did not call for them, the fact must be attributed to the long time he spent abroad, especially in England.... But the abundance of original, genuine German word constructions and uses which we find in Marx in spite of his having spent two-thirds of his life abroad make him highly deserving before the German language, of which he was one of the most prominent masters and creators....

5
Marx the Politician, Scientist and Man

Marx treated politics as a science. Pothouse politicians and politics he loathed. Indeed, can one imagine anything more senseless?

History is the product of all the forces active in man and in nature, of human thought, human passions and human needs. But as a theory, politics is the knowledge of the millions and billions of factors spinning on "the spinning-wheel of time", and as a practice it is action based on that knowledge. Politics is therefore a science and an applied science....

How furious Marx got when he spoke of empty-headed people who thought they could interpret things with a few stereotyped phrases and direct the destinies of the world from a public-house saloon, the newspapers, public meetings or parliaments by taking their more or less muddled wishes and fancies for facts. Luckily the world does not bother about them. Among those "empty heads" there were sometimes quite famous and highly respected "great men".

On this point Marx did not only criticise, he showed a perfect example. In particular in his essays on contemporary developments in France and Napoleon's *coup d'état* and his *New York Daily Tribune* correspondence he provided classical models of the writing of political history.

Here I cannot refrain from a comparison. Bonaparte's *coup d'état*, which Marx dealt with in *The Eighteenth Brumaire*, served Victor Hugo, the greatest of French romantic authors and phrase turners, as the theme of a work which has acquired fame. What a contrast between the two works and the two men! On one side unwieldy grandiloquence and grandiloquent unwieldiness, on the other, systematically arranged facts, the cool-headed scientist weighing facts and the wrathful politician, his judgement unobscured by his wrath.

On the one hand, fleeting sparkling spray, bursts of emotional rhetoric, grotesque caricatures, on the other, each word a well-aimed shaft, each sentence an accusation weighted with facts, the naked truth, overwhelming in its nakedness; no indignation, but plain statement, divulging what actually exists. Victor Hugo's *Napoléon le Petit* had ten editions in quick succession, but today no one remembers it. Marx's *The Eighteenth Brumaire* will be read with admiration thousands of years hence....

Marx could only become what he did become, as I said elsewhere, in England. In a country so undeveloped economically as Germany still was up to the middle of the present century it was just as impossible for Marx to arrive at his criticism of bourgeois economy and the knowledge of the capitalist process of production as for economically undeveloped Germany to have the political institutions of economically developed England. Marx depended just as much on his surroundings and the conditions in which he lived as any other man: without those conditions he would not have become what he is. Nobody proved that better than he did.

To observe such a mind letting conditions act upon it and penetrating deeper and deeper into the nature of society is in itself a profound mental enjoyment. I shall never be able to appreciate at its worth the good fortune that befell me, a young fellow without experience and craving for education, to have Marx as my guide and to profit by his influence and teaching.

Given the many-sidedness, I would go so far as to say the all-embracingness, of his universal mind, a mind that encompassed the universe, penetrated into every substantial detail and never scorned anything as secondary or insignificant, that teaching could not but be many-sided.

Marx was one of the first to grasp the significance of Darwin's research. Even before 1859, the year of the publication of *The Origin of the Species*—and, by a remarkable coincidence, of Marx's *Contribution to the Critique of Political Economy*—Marx realised Darwin's epoch-making importance. For Darwin, in the peace of his country estate far from the hubbub of the city, was preparing a revolution similar to the one which Marx himself was working for in the seething centre of the world. Only the lever was brought to bear on a different point.

Marx kept up with every new appearance and noted every step forward, especially in the fields of natural sciences—including physics and chemistry—and history. The names of Moleschott, Liebig, and Huxley,[1] whose "popular lectures" we attended scrupulously, were as often to be heard among us as those of Ricardo, Adam Smith, MacCulloch[2] and the Scottish and Italian economists. When Darwin drew the conclusions from his research work and brought them to the knowledge of the public, we spoke of nothing

---

[1] *Moleschott, Jacob* (1822-1893)—Dutch-born physiologist, vulgar materialist. *Liebig, Justus* (1803-1873)—outstanding German scientist, one of the founders of agricultural chemistry. *Huxley, Thomas Henry* (1825-1895)—English naturalist, close associate of Charles Darwin and propagator of his theory.—*Ed.*

[2] *Ricardo, David* (1772-1823) and *Smith, Adam* (1723-1790)—English economists, great representatives of classic bourgeois political economy. *MacCulloch, John* (1789-1864)—English bourgeois economist, representative of vulgar political economy.—*Ed.*

else for months but Darwin and the enormous significance of his scientific discoveries....

No one could be kinder and fairer than Marx in giving others their due. He was too great to be envious, jealous or vain. But he had as deadly a hatred for the false greatness and pretended fame of swaggering incapacity and vulgarity as for any kind of deceit and pretence.

Of all the great, little or average men that I have known, Marx is one of the few who were free from vanity. He was too great and too strong to be vain, and too proud as well. He never struck an attitude, he was always himself. He was as incapable as a child of wearing a mask or pretending. As long as social or political grounds did not make it undesirable, he always spoke his mind completely and without any reserve and his face was the mirror of his heart. And when circumstances demanded restraint he showed a sort of childlike awkwardness that often amused his friends.

No man could be more truthful than Marx—he was truthfulness incarnate. Merely by looking at him you knew who it was you were dealing with. In our "civilised" society with its perpetual state of war one cannot always tell the truth, that would be playing into the enemy's hands or risking being sent to Coventry. But even if it is often inadvisable to say the truth, it is not always necessary to say an untruth. I must not always say what I think or feel, but that does not mean that I must say what I do not feel or think. The former is wisdom, the latter hypocrisy. Marx was never a hypocrite. He was absolutely incapable of it, just like an unsophisticated child. His wife often called him "my big baby", and nobody, not even Engels, knew or understood him better than she did. Indeed, when he was in what is generally termed society, where everything is judged by appearances and one must do violence to one's feelings, our "Moor" was like a big boy and he could be embarrassed and blush like a child.

He detested men who acted a part. I still remember how he laughed when he told us of his first meeting with Louis Blanc.[1] He was still living in Dean Street, in the small flat in which there were really only two rooms, the front one,

---

[1] *Blanc, Louis* (1811-1882)—French petty-bourgeois socialist, member of the Provisional Government during the revolution of 1848.—*Ed.*

the parlour, being used as study and reception-room, the back one for everything else. Louis Blanc gave Lenchen his card and she showed him into the front room while Marx quickly dressed in the back room. The door between the two rooms had been left ajar and Marx witnessed an amusing scene. The "great" historian and politician was a very small man, hardly taller than an eight-year-old boy, but he was terribly vain. Looking round the proletarian reception-room, he discovered a very primitive mirror in a corner. He immediately stood in front of it, struck an attitude, stretching his dwarfish stature as much as he could—he had the highest heels I have ever seen—contemplated himself with delight and frisked like a March hare and tried to look imposing. Mrs. Marx, who also witnessed the comic scene, had to bite her lips not to laugh. When he had finished dressing Marx coughed aloud to announce his arrival and give the foppish tribune time to step away from the mirror and welcome his host with a respectful bow. Acting and posing got one nowhere, of course, with Marx, and "little Louis", as the Paris workers called Blanc in contrast to Louis Bonaparte, hastily adopted as natural an attitude as he was capable of....

6

Marx at Work

"Genius is industry," somebody said and it is right to a point, if not completely.

There is no genius without extreme energy and extraordinary hard work. Anything which is called genius and in which neither the former nor the latter has any part is but a shimmering soap bubble or a bill backed by treasures on the moon. Genius is where energy and hard work exceed the average. I have often met people who were considered geniuses by themselves, and sometimes by others too, but had no capacity for work. In reality they were just loafers with a good gift of the gab and talent for publicity. All men of real importance whom I have known were hard workers. This could not be truer than it was of Marx. He was a colossal worker. As he was often prevented from working during the day—especially in the first emigration period—he resorted to night-work. When he came home late from some sitting or meeting it was a regular thing for him to sit down and work a few hours. And the few hours became longer and longer until in the end he worked almost the whole night through and went to sleep in the morning. His wife made earnest reproaches to him about it, but he answered with a laugh that it was in his nature....

Notwithstanding his extraordinarily robust constitution, Marx began to complain of all sorts of troubles at the end of the fifties. A doctor had to be consulted. The result was that Marx was expressly forbidden to work at night. And much exercise—walking and riding—was prescribed. Many were the walks I had with Marx at that time on the outskirts of London, mainly in the hilly north. He soon recovered, too, for his body was indeed made for great exertion and display of strength.

But he hardly felt better when he again gradually fell into his habit of night-work until a crisis came that forced him to adopt a more reasonable mode of life, though only as long as he felt the imperative necessity of it.

The attacks became more and more violent. A liver disease set in, malignant tumours developed. His iron constitution was gradually undermined. I am convinced—and the physicians who last treated him were of the same opinion—that had Marx made up his mind to a life in keeping with nature, that is, with the demands of his organism and of hygiene, he would still be alive today.

Only in his last years, when it was already too late, did he give up working at night. But he worked all the more during the day. He worked whenever it was at all possible to do so. He even had his notebook with him when he went for a walk and kept making entries in it. And his work was never superficial, for there are different ways of working. His was always intense, thorough. His daughter Eleanor gave me a little history table that he drew up for himself to get a general view for some secondary remark. Really nothing was secondary for Marx and the table that he made up for his own temporary use is compiled with as much industry and care as if it had been intended to be printed.

The endurance with which Marx worked often astonished me. He knew no fatigue. Even when he was on the point of breaking down he showed no signs of flagging strength.

If a man's worth is reckoned according to the work he does, as the value of things is reckoned by the amount of work embodied in them, even from that point of view Marx is a man of such value that only a few titanic minds can be compared with him.

What did bourgeois society give Marx in recompense for that enormous quantity of work?

Capital cost Marx forty years' work, and work such as Marx alone was capable of. I shall not be exaggerating if I say that the lowest paid day-labourer in Germany got more pay in forty years than Marx as honorarium or, to put it bluntly, as debt of honour for one of the two greatest scientific creations of the century. The other one is Darwin's work.

"Science" is not a marketable value. And bourgeois society cannot be expected to pay a reasonable price for the drawing up of its own death sentence....

7

In the House in Dean Street

From summer 1850 to the beginning of 1862 when I returned to Germany I went to Marx's house almost every day and for many years stayed there the whole day. I was just like one of the family....

Before Marx moved into the cottage in Maitland Park Road he lived in a modest flat in unpretentious Dean Street, Soho Square—a homing point for travellers, people passing through and emigrants of all kinds, and there was a continual coming and going of not so important, more important and most important people. Besides, it was the natural meeting-place for the comrades whose fixed residence was in London. As far as fixed residence went there was always some hitch, for in London it was difficult to get a regular lodging. Hunger made most of the emigrants leave for the provinces or even for America. It made short work with some of them and sent the wretched emigrant to one of the London cemeteries where it gave him a place to rest, if not to live in. But I managed to hold out and, excepting

Chartist demonstration in May 1842

First revolutionary battles of the proletariat. Uprising of Lyons weavers in 1834

the faithful Lessner and Lochner,[1] who, however, rarely came to Dean Street, I was the only one of the London "community" who went in and out of "Moor's" house like one of the family during the whole of the emigration period except a short time that I shall mention in my sketches. I was therefore able to see and find out what others could not.

8
Emigrants' Intrigues

My friends and comrades of the time before I went to London often made fun of me because of my attachment to Marx. Quite recently I found a letter sent to me in that period by Bauer from Sinsheim, one of the most efficient Baden volunteers.[2] He died a few years ago in Milwaukee where he was editor of a radical-democratic paper which he himself founded. Like most of the emigrants who had the means to do so, he had left for the United States after a short stay in London and soon found work to suit him in the press.

That was the most difficult period for the London emigrants and Bauer was very keen on having me with him. He had already sent me several letters offering me reliable prospects of a reasonable salary as an editor. At the time I had not even a crust to whet my teeth on and the fifty dollars a week that I was offered was a most attractive bait. But I resisted, not wishing to be any farther from the battlefield than was necessary, for I knew that whoever crossed the ocean had 999 chances out of 1,000 of being lost to Europe.

Finally, Bauer resorted to the last weapon by tickling my self-love. In a letter which I still have in my papers he wrote:

---

[1] *Lessner, Friedrich* (1825-1910)—active figure in the international working-class movement; tailor by trade; associate and friend of Marx and Engels. *Lochner, Georg* (born c. 1824)—active participant in the German working-class movement, member of the Communist League and the First International; carpenter by trade; supporter and friend of Marx and Engels.—*Ed.*

[2] Karl Friedrich Bauer, who took part in the Baden-Pfalz rising in 1849.—*Ed.*

"Here you will be a free man, you can achieve a lot independently. But what are you over there? A play-ball, an ass used as a beast of burden and then laughed at. What is it like in your heavenly kingdom? At the top thrones the all-knowing, the all-wise, the Dalai Lama, Marx. Then a big gap. Then comes Engels. And then a great big gap again. Then Wolff. Then another big gap. And then, perhaps, the 'sentimental ass', Liebknecht.". . .

I answered that I had no objection to coming after people who had done more than I, that I preferred to be in company of men from whom I could learn something and whom I could look up to rather than of men I would have to look down upon, as upon all his "great men".

So I stayed where I was, and learned.

But that was the opinion that emigrants outside our circle had of Marx and our society. It excited their imagination that we had shut ourselves off from them so completely and they made up a maze of myths and gossip. But we did not let that worry us.

9

Meetings at Marx's

Marx's wife had perhaps just as much influence on my development as Marx himself. My mother died when I was three years old and I was brought up in a rather hard way.... In Marx's wife I met a beautiful, noble-minded and intelligent woman who was half sister, half mother to the friendless, lonely volunteer rebel washed up on the banks of the Thames. I am persuaded that it was my association with Marx's family that saved me from ruin in the distresses of emigration....

I should have neither time nor room enough to introduce all the people that I met during that time in Marx's house and company. Besides the German and other emigrants from whom no hostility of principle separated us, I met the leaders of the English working-class movement, the spartanic Julian Harney, the eloquent tribune and ardent journalist Ernest Jones, the last two great representatives of Chartism[1]

---

[1] *Chartism*—first mass revolutionary movement of the English working class (1830s and 1840s).—*Ed.*

which grew into socialism; Frost who was condemned to life
deportation for being at the head of the Chartist rising but
was pardoned and returned to England in the fifties, the
most remarkable of the "physical force men",[1] and Robert
Owen, the aged patriarch of socialism, by far the most comprehensive, penetrating and practical of all the predecessors
of scientific socialism. We were at the gathering to celebrate
his eightieth birthday and I had the good fortune to visit
him frequently at his house....

Shortly after me a French working man came to London.
He aroused a lively interest not only in the French colony,
but in all us emigrants and also in our "shadows"—the international police. His name was Barthélémy. We had read
in the papers of his clever and daring escape from the Conciergerie. Rather above average height, strong and muscular,
with coal-black curly hair and sparkling black eyes, he
was a typical southern Frenchman and the very personification of determination.

His proud head was surrounded with a legendary halo. He
had been sentenced to the galleys and had the indelible
brand on his shoulder. When he was only seventeen years
old he killed a policeman during the Blanqui-Barbès insurrection in 1839[2] and was sent to a convict colony. Amnestied
at the February Revolution in 1848, he returned to Paris
and took part in all the movements and demonstrations of
the proletariat. He fought in the June battle.[3] He was captured at one of the last barricades but was fortunately not
recognised by anybody in the first days; otherwise he would
certainly have been "summarily" shot like so many others.
The first violence had ebbed when he was brought before a
military court and he was only condemned to "the dry guillotine", that is, to life deportation to Cayenne. For some
reason his case was held up and in June 1850 he was still
in the Conciergerie. Just before his deportation to the land
where pepper grows and men die he succeeded in escaping.

---

[1] The Left, revolutionary trend in the Chartist movement, which favoured physical violence in opposition to the "moral force men" who wished to keep the movement within the bounds of peaceful agitation. —*Ed*.
[2] The insurrection of the Blanquist secret revolutionary Seasons of the Year Society in Paris, May 1839.—*Ed*.
[3] The June insurrection of the Paris proletariat in 1848.—*Ed*.

He naturally went to London, where he entered into a close association with us and was often at Marx's....

I frequently fought him—I mean it literally. The French emigrants had set up a "sword room" in Rathbone Place, Oxford Street, where one could practise fencing with sabre or sword and pistol shooting. Marx occasionally went there and had some strenuous fights with the Frenchmen. He tried to make up for his lack of skill by impetuosity and he sometimes bluffed those who were not cool enough. The French are known to use the sword for a thrust as well as for a cut, and that disconcerts Germans at first, but one soon gets used to it. Barthélémy was a good swordsman and he often practised with the pistol so that before long he was an excellent marksman. He soon got into Willich's[1] company and conceived hatred for Marx.

The difference with Willich's sect became bitterer and one evening Marx was challenged to a duel by Willich. Marx treated that Prussian officer trick for what it was worth, but young Conrad Schramm,[2] a hotspur, replied by insulting Willich, who challenged him in accordance with his student code. The duel was to take place by the coast in Belgium, pistols being chosen as the weapon. Schramm had never held a pistol in his hand before, whereas Willich never missed the ace of hearts at twenty paces. His second was Barthélémy. We were afraid for our dashing chivalrous Schramm.

The day appointed for the duel went by, we counting the minutes. Next evening, when Marx was away and only his wife and Lenchen were at home, the door opened and Barthélémy entered. He bowed stiffly and in answer to the anxious request for news announced in a sepulchral tone: "*Schramm a une balle dans la tête*"—Schramm has a bullet in the head! Then he bowed stiffly again, wheeled round and went out. The fright of Mrs. Marx, who almost lost consciousness, can easily be imagined.... An hour later she told us the bad news. We naturally gave up all hope for Schramm.

---

[1] There was a split in the Communist League in 1850. Willich and Schapper headed the "Left" adventuristic group which was expelled from the League.—*Ed.*

[2] *Schramm, Conrad* (1822-1858)—German revolutionary; member of the Communist League, friend of Marx and Engels.—*Ed.*

Next day, just as we were all talking about him mournfully, the door opened and in came the man we thought dead, his head bandaged, but laughing merrily. He told us that the bullet had grazed him and he had lost consciousness. When he had recovered he had been alone by the seashore with his second and the doctor. Willich and Barthélemy had just managed to catch a boat back from Ostend. Schramm left on the next. . . .

10
Marx and Children

Like every strong and healthy nature, Marx had an extraordinary love for children. He was not only a most loving father who could be a child for hours with his children, he felt drawn as by a magnet towards other children, especially helpless ones in distress whom he came across. Hundreds of times he left us as we were going through poor districts to go and pat the head of some child sitting in rags on the door-step and press a penny or a halfpenny into its hand. He distrusted beggars, for begging had become a regular trade in London, and one that paid too, even if only coppers at a time. Consequently Marx was not long taken in by men or women who went begging, though at first he never refused alms if he had any money. If any of them tried artfully to move him by feigning illness or need he was profoundly angry with them, for he considered the exploitation of human pity especially base and equivalent to stealing from the poor. But if a man or woman with a weeping child came to Marx begging, he could not resist the entreating eyes of the child, no matter how clearly roguery was written on the face of the man or woman. . . .

He would have enjoyed having a man who beat his wife—which was common at the time in London—flogged to death. In such cases his impulsive nature often got him and us in trouble.

One evening he and I were going to Hampstead Road on the top of a bus. At a stop by a public-house there was a great hubbub and a woman could be heard screaming: "Murder! Murder!" Marx was down in a trice and I followed him. I tried to keep him back but I might just as well have tried to stop a bullet with my hand. We immediately found ourselves in the middle of the tumult with people pressing behind us. "What's the matter?" It was all too obvious what the matter was. A drunken woman had quarrelled with her husband, he wanted to take her home and she was resisting, shouting like one possessed. So far so good. As we saw, there was no reason for us to interfere. But the quarrelling couple saw it too and immediately made peace and went for us. The crowd around us grew and pressed closer and adopted a threatening attitude to the "damned foreigners". The woman, in particular, attacked Marx, making his fine black beard the object of her rage. I tried to calm the storm, but in vain. Only the arrival of two stalwart constables saved us from paying dearly for our philanthropic interference. We were glad when we were safe and sound on an omnibus again, on our way home. Later Marx was more cautious in his attempts to interfere in such cases....

One had to see Marx with his children to have an idea of his profound affection and simplicity. When he had a minute to spare or during his walks he would run about with them and take part in their merriest, most boisterous games: he was like a child among children. Occasionally we would play "cavalry" on Hampstead Heath. I would take one of the daughters on my shoulders and Marx the other, and then a jumping competition or races would start or the riders would fight a cavalry battle. The girls were as wild as boys and it took more than a bump to make them cry.

Jennychen, the elder of the two girls, was the very image of her father: she had the same black eyes, the same forehead. She sometimes had pythonic transports: "the spirit came over her," as over Pythia. Her eyes would begin to shine and blaze and she would start declaiming, often the most astonishing fantasies. She had one of those fits one day on the way home from Hampstead Heath and spoke of life on the stars, her account taking the form of poetry. Mrs. Marx, in her maternal anxiety, several of her children having died young, said: "Children of her age do not say things like that, her precocity is a sign of bad health." But Moor scolded her and I showed her Pythia, who had recovered from her prophetic trance, skipping about and laughing merrily, the very picture of health....

Both Marx's sons died young, one, who was born in London, when still very young, the other, born in Brussels, after a long infirmity. The death of the latter was a terrible blow for Marx. I still remember the sad weeks of the hopeless disease. The boy, named Edgar after an uncle but called "*Mush*", was very gifted but sickly from birth, a real child of sorrow. He had beautiful eyes and a promising head which seemed too heavy for his weak body. Poor Mush might have lived if he had had peace and constant care and had lived in the country or by the seaside. But in emigration, hunted from place to place and amid the hardships of London life, even the tenderest parental affection and motherly care could not give the frail plant the strength it needed to fight for its life. Mush died....

I cannot forget the scene: the mother weeping in silence bending over her dead child, Lenchen standing by and sobbing, and Marx, in the grip of a terrible agitation, answering violently and almost wrathfully any attempt to console him, the two girls weeping silently and pressing close to their mother who clung feverishly to them as if to defend them against death which had robbed her of her boys.

The burial took place two days later. Lessner, Pfänder,[1] Lochner, Conrad Schramm, Red Wolff[2] and I attended. I went in the coach with Marx. He sat there without a word, his head in his hands....

Later Tussy was born, a merry little thing, as round as a ball and like cream and roses, first wheeled about in her perambulator, then sometimes carried and sometimes toddling along. She was six years old when I came back to Germany, just half the age of my eldest daughter, who in the previous two years had accompanied the Marx family on their Sunday walks to Hampstead Heath.

Marx could not do without the society of children, which was his rest and refreshment. When his own children were

---

[1] *Pfänder, Karl* (c. 1818-1876)—active member of the German working-class movement, member of the Central Committee of the Communist League and the General Council of the First International; artist; supporter of Marx and Engels.—*Ed.*

[2] Nickname for Ferdinand Wolff, member of the Communist League and an editor of the *Neue Rheinische Zeitung* in 1848-49.—*Ed.*

grown up or had died his grandchildren took their place. Jennychen, who married Longuet, one of the Commune emigrants, at the beginning of the seventies, brought Marx several turbulent grandsons. Jean or Johnny, the eldest... and the most turbulent, was his grandfather's favourite. He could do what he liked with him and he knew it.

One day when I was on a visit to London, Johnny, whose parents had sent him over from Paris, as they did several times a year, got the idea of using his grandfather as an omnibus and riding on top, i.e., on Moor's shoulders, Engels and I being the horses. When we were properly harnessed there was a wild chase,—I was going to say drive—round the little garden behind Marx's cottage in Maitland Park Road. Or perhaps it was at Engels' house in Regent Park Road, for London houses are all very much alike and it is easy to confuse them, and still more the gardens. A few square yards of gravel and grass covered with "black snow" or London soot so that you cannot tell where the gravel ends and the grass begins—that is what a London "garden" is like.

The ride started: Gee-ho! with international—English, German, and French—shouts: "Go on! *Plus vite!* Hurrah!" And Moor had to trot until the sweat dripped from his brow. When Engels or I tried to slow down a little the merciless coachman's whip lashed down on us: "You naughty horse! *En avant!*" And it went on until Marx was dropping and then we had to parley with Johnny and a truce was concluded....

11

Lenchen

Ever since the Marx family was founded Lenchen had been the life and soul of the house, as one of the daughters put it.... All the work she had to do! And she did it all gladly.... Always good-humoured, smiling, ready to help. And yet she could get angry, and she hated Moor's enemies bitterly.

When Mrs. Marx was ill or out of sorts Lenchen replaced her as a mother, and in any case she was a second mother to the children. She had great strength and steadfastness of will: if she considered something necessary it just had to be done.

As has already been said, Lenchen was a kind of dictator in the house: to put it more exactly, Lenchen was the dictator but Mrs. Marx was the mistress. And Marx submitted as meekly as a lamb to that dictatorship.

No man is great in the eyes of his servant, it is said. And Marx was certainly not in Lenchen's eyes. She would have sacrificed herself for him, she would have given her life a hundred times for him, Mrs. Marx or any of the children had it been necessary and possible. She did, indeed, give her life for them. But Marx could not impose on her. She knew him with all his whims and weaknesses and she could twist him round her little finger. Even when he was irritated and stormed and thundered so that nobody else would go near him, Lenchen would go into the lion's den. If he growled at her, Lenchen would give him such a piece of her mind that the lion became as mild as a lamb.

12

Walks with Marx

Those walks to Hampstead Heath! Were I to live to a thousand I would never forget them.

The Heath is on the other side of Primrose Hill and like the latter it is well known to non-Londoners from Dickens' Pickwickians. Most of it is not built up even today, it is still a hilly heath covered with gorse and bushes and miniature mountains and valleys where anyone can stroll and frolic as he likes without fear of being served a summons by a keeper for trespassing. It is still a favourite resort of Londoners and when Sunday is fine the heath is black with men and colourful with women. The latter have a special liking for trying the patience of the admittedly very patient donkeys and horses you can ride there. Forty years ago Hampstead Heath was much larger and less artificial than now and a Sunday there was our greatest treat.

The children used to speak about it the whole week and even the adults, young and old, looked forward to it. The journey there was a treat in itself. The girls were excellent walkers, as nimble and tireless as cats. From Dean Street, where the Marxes lived—quite near Church Street where I had settled down—it was a good hour and a half away and we generally set out at about eleven o'clock. Not always, however, for in London people do not get up early and by the time everything was in order, the children seen to and the hamper packed properly it was much later.

That hamper! It hovers before "my mind's eye" as real and material, attractive and appetising as if it was only yesterday I had seen Lenchen carrying it.

When a healthy and vigorous person has not much coppers in his pocket (and it was no question of silver then) food is a thing of primary importance. Our good Lenchen knew that and her kind heart pitied her poor guests, who went short often enough and were therefore always hungry. A substantial joint of roast veal was the main course, consecrated by tradition for the Sunday outings to Hampstead Heath. A basket of a size quite unusual in London, brought by Lenchen from Trier, was the tabernacle in which the holy of holies was borne. Then there was tea and sugar and occasionally some fruit. Bread and cheese could be bought on the heath, where crockery, hot water and milk were also to be had, just as in a Berlin Kafféegarten. Besides you could get as much butter and, according to the local custom, shrimps, watercress and periwinkles, as you wanted and could afford....

The walk there took place as follows. I generally led the way with the two girls, entertaining them with stories or acrobatics or picking wild flowers, which were more abundant then than now. Behind us came a few friends and then the main body: Marx with his wife and one of the Sunday visitors who was deserving of special consideration. In the rear came Lenchen and the hungriest of our party, who helped her to carry the hamper. If there were more people in our company they were distributed among the different groups. Needless to say, the order of battle or march varied according to need or desire.

When we arrived at the Heath we first of all chose a place to pitch our tent, taking tea and beer facilities into consideration as much as possible.

Once food and drink had been partaken of, both sexes went in search of the most comfortable place to lie or sit.

Then those who did not prefer a nap got out the Sunday papers bought on the way and spoke about politics. The children soon found playmates and played hide-and-seek among the gorse bushes.

But there had to be variety even in those pleasant occupations: races, wrestling, heaving stones and other forms of sport were organised. One Sunday we discovered a chestnut-tree with ripe nuts near by.

"Let's see who can bring the most down," somebody said, and we went at it with a cheer. Marx was as tireless as any of us. Not till the last nut was brought down did the bombardment stop. Marx was unable to move his right arm for a week and I was not much better off.

The best treat was when we all went for a donkey ride. How we laughed and joked! And what comical figures we cut! Marx had fun himself and gave us plenty, twice as much as himself; his horsemanship was so primitive and he exerted such fantasy to assure us of his skill! And his skill boiled down to having taken riding lessons once when he was a student—Engels maintained that he had never got further than the third lesson—and on his rare visits to Manchester he went riding a venerable Rosinante, probably a great-grandchild of the placid mare that the late old Fritz presented to the brave Gellert.[1]

The walk home from Hampstead Heath was always a merry one, although the pleasure ahead gladdened us more than the one behind. We had grounds enough for melancholy, but we were charmed against it by our grim humour. Emigration misery did not exist for us; whoever started to complain was immediately most forcibly reminded of his duties to society.

The marching order for the return was not the same as going. The children were tired with the day's running and they brought up the rearguard with Lenchen, who, light-footed now that the hamper was empty, could take care of them. Generally someone struck up a song. We seldom sang political songs, ours were mostly folk songs, full of feeling and "patriotism"—it is not a hunter's yarn I am telling—of the *"Vaterland"* like *O Strassburg, O Strassburg, du wunder-*

---

[1] *Fritz*—King Frederick II of Prussia. *Gellert*—poet of the court.—*Ed.*

schöne Stadt, which was especially popular. Or the children would sing us Negro songs and dance to them when their feet were not so weary. As little was said about politics while walking as about the misery of emigration. But literature and art were frequent topics, which gave Marx the opportunity of showing his astonishing memory. He used to recite long passages from *The Divine Comedy,*[1] which he knew almost by heart, and scenes from Shakespeare. His wife, whose knowledge of Shakespeare was excellent, often recited instead of him....

After we moved to Kentish Town and Haverstock Hill in the north of London at the end of the fifties our favourite outings were to the meadows and hills between and beyond Hampstead and Highgate. There we used to look for flowers and explain plants, which was a double joy for town children who developed a yearning for green nature as a result of the cold, tumultuous stony sea of the city. What a pleasure it was for us to discover on one of our ramblings a small pool in the shadow of some trees and when I was able to show the children the first "wild" forget-me-not. Still greater was our pleasure when, after careful spying out of the ground, we disregarded the "No Trespassing" signs and went on to a velvety dark-green meadow and found hyacinths and other spring flowers in a spot sheltered from the wind.... At first I could not believe my eyes, for I had learned that hyacinths grew wild only in southerly countries—in Switzerland by the Lake of Geneva, in Italy and Greece, but no farther north. Here was a palpable proof of the contrary and an unexpected corroboration of the English assertion that as far as flora is concerned England has the same climate as Italy. There was no doubt about it: they were hyacinths, ordinary, greyish blue ones, the flowers not so big as the garden hyacinth, and not so many of them on a single stem, but with the same smell, though somewhat more stringent....

We looked down from our fragrant Asphodel meadows proudly upon the world, the mighty boundless city of the world which lay before us in its vastness, shrouded in the ugly mystery of the fog.

---

[1] By the great Italian poet Dante.—*Ed.*

13
An Unpleasant Quarter of an Hour

Who does not know Rabelais'[1] unpleasant quarter of an hour, during which we must foot the bill or something worse will happen? Who has not had such bad quarters of an hour? I have. Before an examination, before my first speech, the first time I was ordered by the warder in front of the prison door to hand in my braces and tie, to prevent me, as I was told with unreserved frankness in answer to my puzzled question, from avoiding court-martial by suicide. Those and others were certainly unpleasant quarters of an hour. But they were pleasant in comparison with the one I want to tell about. That was not even a quarter of an hour. It was at the most half a quarter of an hour. Perhaps no more than five minutes. I did not measure the time, I had no time to do so. And even if I had had time, I had no watch. An emigrant with a watch! All I know is that it was an eternity for me.

It happened on November 18, 1852, in London.

Lord Wellington, the Iron Duke and "victor in a hundred battles", but softened and tamed by the English people during the Reform movement, had died in his castle at Walmer on September 14 ... and the "national funeral" of the "national hero" was to take place with "national pomp" in St. Paul's, where he was to be buried beside other "national heroes". Since the day of his death, that is for about two months, all England and especially all London had been talking of the ceremony which was to surpass all previous national solemnities in pomp and magnificence just as the duke himself was claimed by the English to have surpassed all previous heroes.... The day had arrived. The whole of England was in movement, the whole of London was afoot. Hundreds of thousands had come up to the capital, thousands had come from abroad adding to the millions in the giant city itself.

I hate such shows and tumultuous crowds, and like many of my fellow-emigrants I would have preferred to stay at

---

[1] *Rabelais, François* (c. 1494-1553)—great French humanist writer of the Renaissance.—*Ed.*

home or go to St. James's Park. But two female friends overcame the firmness of my decision....

They were indeed great friends of mine—dark-eyed, black curly-headed Jenny, the very image of Moor, her father, and delicate, fair-headed Laura with the roguish eyes, the cheery image of her mother....

Both of them had taken to me on our first meeting and they always claimed me as soon as I appeared. They were largely responsible for my keeping, during my life of exile in London, the good humour to which I owe my life. How often, when I was at my wit's end, did I flee to my little friends and ramble with them through the streets and parks. My melancholy thoughts were at once dispelled and a more pleasant mood gave me joy and strength for the struggle.

Generally I had to tell them stories, for I had soon received acknowledgement as a good story-teller and was always greeted with boisterous joy. Luckily I knew a lot of tales, but when my stock was exhausted I had to make up more....

"Do take care of the children," Mrs. Marx said to me, as I left for the show with the impatiently tripping girls. "Don't go where the crowd's too thick." And when we were at the door, Lenchen, running anxiously after us, shouted: "Be careful now, Library, there's a good fellow!" (Library was a puzzling nickname the children had given me.)...

I had my plan ready. We had no money to pay for a place at a window or on a stand. As the procession was to go via the Strand and along the river, the thing to do was to go down one of the streets leading from the Strand down to the river.

The girls were holding my hand on either side, I had a snack in my pocket. We made our way towards the spot I had decided on—not far from Temple Bar and the old city gates between Westminster and the City. The streets had been full of people all morning and were now crowded, but as the procession had to pass through remote districts of the capital the crowd branched off along different streets and we reached the point I had in view without any jostling. My choice turned out to be a good one. We took up our places on a flight of steps, the two girls standing a step higher than me, holding on to my hand and clinging tight to each other.

What was that? The crowd swayed. A distant, swelling clamour like the dull roar of the ocean came nearer and nearer.... The children were delighted. There was no crush, all my anxiety was dispelled.

A long time the gold-sparkling procession passed in front of us in an endless succession until the last goldbraided rider went past and it was over.

Suddenly the crowd massed behind us lurched forward, eager to follow the procession. I planted my feet as firmly as I could and tried to protect the children so that the crowd could sweep past without touching them. In vain. No human strength could stand up to the elemental force of the masses any more than a fragile boat can break the ice-floes after a rigorous winter. I had to give way, and holding the girls tight against me I tried to get out of the main stream. I thought I had succeeded and was breathing relieved when another more powerful human wave bore down on us from the right: we were swept into the Strand and the thousands of people who had massed there pressed on behind the *cortège* in order to enjoy the sight again. I clenched my teeth and tried to lift the girls on to my shoulders but the crowd was pressing me too closely. I grabbed madly at the children's arms but the whirlwind carried us on. Suddenly I felt a force wedging in between the children and myself. The children were wrenched away from me. Resistance was in vain. I had to leave hold of them for fear their arms would be broken or dislocated. It was a moment of anguish.

What could I do? Temple Bar Gate rose in front with its three passages: one in the middle for vehicles, one on either side for pedestrians. The human tide eddied against the gate like waters against the pillars of a bridge. I had to get through! The fearful cries all around me impressed on me the nature of the danger. If the children were not trampled underfoot I would find them on the other side where the pressure would be eased up. How I hoped it would be so!

I worked furiously with elbows and chest. But in such a tide a single man is like a straw in a whirlpool. I struggled and struggled. Dozens of times I thought I was through, but was swept aside. At last there was a jerk, a terrible crush, and in a moment I was on the other side, free of the densest throng. I sought feverishly here and there. Not there! My heart was gripped in a vice. Then two clear children's voices: "Library!" I thought I was dreaming. It was like the music of angels. The two girls stood before me, smiling and unharmed. I kissed them and fondled them. For a minute I was speechless. Then they told me how the human wave that had wrenched them out of my grasp had carried them safely through the gate and thrown them aside under the cover of the very walls that had caused the bottleneck on the other side. There, remembering my instructions to remain where they were as far as possible if ever they got lost on any of our outings, they had clung to a projection in the wall.

We went home with a feeling of triumph. Mrs. Marx, Moor and Lenchen welcomed us with joy, for they had been very uneasy. They had heard that the crowd had been terrible and that many people had been crushed and hurt. The children had no idea of the danger in which they had been, they had enjoyed it immensely. And I did not say that evening what a terrible quarter of an hour I had been through.

Several women had lost their lives at the very spot where the children had been torn away from me.

I can remember that bad quarter of an hour as vividly as if it had been yesterday....

14

Marx and Chess

Marx was an excellent draughts player. He was so expert at the game that it was difficult to beat him at all. He enjoyed chess too, but he was not so skilful at it. He tried to make up for that by zeal and surprise attacks.

Chess was popular among us emigrants at the beginning of the fifties. We had more time and, although "time is money", less money than we could have wished for. We therefore engaged a lot in the "game of the wise" under the direction of Red Wolff who had frequented the best chess

Hélène Demuth

Paul Lafargue

Friedrich Lessner

H. A. Lopatin

circles in Paris and learned something about it. Sometimes we had heated chess contests. The one who lost came in for plenty of banter and the games were merry and often very noisy.

When Marx was in a tight corner he got vexed, and when he lost a game he was furious. In the Model Lodging-House[1] in Old Compton Street, where several of us lodged for a time for 3/6 a week, we were always surrounded by Englishmen watching the game with keen interest—chess was popular in England, among the workers too—greatly amused by our boisterous good humour, for two Germans are noisier than a couple of dozen Englishmen.

One day Marx triumphantly informed us that he had discovered a new move that would lick all of us. His challenge was accepted. True enough, he beat us all one after the other. But we soon learned from our defeat and I succeeded in checkmating Marx. It was already quite late, so he insisted on a return game next day at his house.

At eleven sharp—quite early for London—I was at Marx's house. He was not in his room, but I was told he would soon be coming. Mrs. Marx was not to be seen and Lenchen was not in a very good humour. Before I could ask what was the matter, Moor came in, shook hands with me and got the chess-board out. Then the fight began. Marx had improved on his move during the night, and before long I was in a hopeless position. I was checkmated and Marx was delighted. He ordered something to drink and some sandwiches. Then we had another game and I won. We played on with varying luck and a varying mood.... Mrs. Marx kept out of sight and none of the children dared to come near. The contest raged, favouring now one, then the other. At last I beat Marx twice running. He insisted on continuing, but Lenchen said peremptorily: "Enough of it!"....

---

[1] A barracks-like building with rooms for lodgers, a common kitchen and sitting-room and a reading and smoking room. There were a number of such lodging-houses in London. Some had lodgings with several rooms for families and besides the common rooms already mentioned there was a common wash-room. These institutions were run by a special steward and were kept scrupulously clean. Several are still run with success in London. (*Note by Liebknecht.—Ed.*)

15
Privation and Hardship

An incredible number of lies have been told about Marx, among other things that he lived a life of revelry and riot while the majority of emigrants around him were starving. I do not claim the right to go into details, but I can say this much: Mrs. Marx's notes have given me repeated and vivid proof that Marx and his family did not experience mere isolated instances of the hardship that can befall any emigrant in a foreign country, deprived of all support, but that they suffered the severest privations of life in emigration for years. There were probably not many emigrants who suffered more than the Marx family. Later, when his income was larger and more regular, they were still not assured against want. For years, even after the worst was over, the pound that Marx got every week for his articles in the *New York Daily Tribune* was his only guaranteed income....

16
Illness and Death of Marx
(Tussy's Letter)[1]

"All I can tell you about Moor's stay in Mustapha (Algiers) is that the weather was shocking, that Moor found a very nice and capable doctor there and that everybody in the hotel was friendly and attentive towards him.

"During the autumn and winter of 1881-82 Moor first stayed with Jenny at Argenteuil, near Paris. We met him there and stayed a few weeks. Then he went to the south of France and to Algiers, but he was not well when he came back. He spent the autumn and winter of 1882-83 in Ventnor, Isle of Wight, returning in January 1883 after Jenny's death.

"Now about Karlsbad. We went there for the first time in 1874, when Moor was sent there because of liver trouble

---

[1] Liebknecht here quotes a letter he received from Marx's youngest daughter Eleanor (Tussy).—*Ed.*

and sleeplessness. As his first stay there did him extraordinary good he went again by himself in 1875. In the following year, 1876, I went with him again because he said he had missed me too much the preceding year. In Karlsbad he was most conscientious about his cure, scrupulously doing everything prescribed for him. We made many friends there. Moor was a charming travelling companion. He was always in a good humour and ready to take pleasure in everything—a beautiful landscape or a glass of beer. And his immense knowledge of history made every place we went to more living and present in the past than in the present itself.

"I think a certain amount has been written on Moor's stay in Karlsbad. I heard, among other things, of a fairly long article but I cannot remember what paper it was in.

"In 1874 we saw you in Leipzig. On our return we made a detour to Bingen, which Moor wanted to show me because he was there with my mother on their honeymoon. On these two journeys we also visited Dresden, Berlin, Prague, Hamburg and Nuremberg.

"In 1877 Moor was to go to Karlsbad again but we were informed that the German and Austrian authorities intended to expel him, and as the journey was too long and expensive to risk an expulsion he did not go there any more. This was a great disadvantage for him, for after his cure he always felt rejuvenated.

"Our main reason for going to Berlin was to see my father's faithful friend, my dear Uncle Edgar von Westphalen. We only stayed there a couple of days. Moor was greatly amused to hear that the police went to our hotel on the third day, just an hour after we had left."

* * *

"By autumn 1881 our dear *Mömchen* (mother) was so ill that she could rarely leave her sick bed. Moor had a severe attack of pleurisy, the result of his having neglected his ailments. The doctor, our good friend Donkin, considered his case almost hopeless. That was a terrible time. Our dear Mother lay in the big front room, Moor in the small room next to it. They who were so used to each other, whose lives had come to form part of each other, could not even be together in the same room any longer.

"Our good old Lenchen,—you know what she was to us—and I had to nurse them both. The doctor said it was our nursing that saved Moor. However that may be, I only know that neither Lenchen nor I went to bed for three weeks. We were on our feet day and night and when we were too exhausted we would rest an hour in turns.

"Moor got the better of his illness again. Never shall I forget the morning he felt himself strong enough to go into Mother's room. When they were together they were young again—she a young girl and he a loving youth, both on life's threshold, not an old disease-ridden man and an old dying woman parting from each other for life.

"Moor got better, and although he was not yet strong, he seemed to be regaining strength.

"Then Mother died on December 2, 1881. Her last words —a remarkable thing was that they were in English—were addressed to her 'Karl'.

"When our dear General (Engels) came he said something that nearly made me wild at him:

" 'Moor is dead too.'

"And it was true.

"When our dear Mother passed away, so did Moor. He fought hard to hang on to life, for he was a fighter to the end—but he was a broken man. His general condition got worse and worse. Had he been selfish he would have let things go as they wished. But for him one thing was above everything else—his devotedness to the cause. He tried to complete his great work and that was why he agreed to another journey for his health.

"In spring 1882 he went to Paris and Argenteuil, where I met him. We spent a few really happy days with Jenny and her children. Then Moor went to the south of France and finally to Algiers.

"During the whole of his stay in Algiers, Nice and Cannes the weather was bad. He wrote me long letters from Algiers. I lost many of them because I sent them to Jenny at his wish and she did not send me many back.

"When Moor finally returned home he was very poorly and we began to fear the worst. On the advice of the doctors he spent the autumn and winter in Ventnor on the Isle of Wight. Here I must mention that at Moor's wish I spent three months at that time in Italy with Jenny's eldest son Jean (Johnny). At the beginning of 1883 I went to Moor, taking Johnny with me, for he was his favourite grandson. I was obliged to return because I had lessons to give.

"Then came the last terrible blow: the news of Jenny's death. Jenny, Moor's first-born, the daughter he loved the most, died suddenly (on January 11). We had had letters from Moor—I have them in front of me now—telling us that Jenny's health was improving and that we (Hélène and I) need not be anxious. The telegram informing us of her death arrived an hour after that letter of Moor. I immediately left for Ventnor.

"I have lived many a sad hour, but none so sad as that. I felt that I was bringing my father his death sentence. I racked my brain all the long anxious way to find how I could break the news to him. But I did not need to, my face gave me away. Moor said at once: 'Our Jennychen is dead.' Then he urged me to go to Paris at once and help with the children. I wanted to stay with him but he brooked no resistance. I had hardly been half an hour at Ventnor when I set out again on the sad journey to London. From there I left for Paris. I was doing what Moor wanted me to do for the sake of the children.

"I shall not say anything about my return home. I can only think with a shudder of that time, the anguish, the torment. But enough of that....

"A few more words about our dear Mother. She was dying for months, bearing the appalling tortures that cancer brings with it. And yet her good humour, her inexhaustible wit that you know so well never left her a minute. She asked with the impatience of a child about the results of the elections in Germany (1881). And how she rejoiced at the victory! She was cheerful to her very death, trying to dispel our anxiety for her with jokes. Yes, she who was suffering so terribly actually joked and laughed at the doctor and all of us because we were so serious. She was conscious almost till the last minute, and when she could no longer speak—her last words were for 'Karl'—she squeezed our hands and tried to smile.

"As far as Moor is concerned, you know that he went out of his bedroom to his study in Maitland Park, sat down in his armchair and calmly passed away.

"The 'General' had that armchair until he died. Now I have got it.

"When you write about Moor do not forget Lenchen. I know you will not forget Mother. Hélène was in a way the axis on which everything in the house revolved. She was the best and most faithful friend. So do not forget Hélène when you write about Moor."

* * *

"I shall now give you some details about Moor's stay in the south as you asked me to. At the beginning of 1882 he and I stayed a few weeks with Jenny at Argenteuil. In March and April Moor was in Algiers, in May in Monte Carlo, Nice and Cannes. He was at Jenny's again about the end of June and the whole of July. Lenchen was also at Argenteuil then. From there he went to Switzerland, Vevey and so on, with Laura. Towards the end of September or beginning of October, he returned to England and went straight to Ventnor, where Johnny and I went to see him.

"Now for a few notes in answer to your questions. Our little Edgar (Mush) was born in 1847, I think, and died in April 1855. Little Fawkes (Heinrich) was born on November 5, 1849, and died when he was about two.[1] My sister Franzisca was born in 1851 and died while still a baby, at about eleven months."

* * *

"You asked some questions about our good Hélène, or 'Nym', as we called her towards the end, Johnny Longuet having given her the name for some reason unknown to me

---

[1] He was called Fawkes after Guy Fawkes, hero of the "gunpowder plot". (*Note by Liebknecht.*) On November 5, 1605, the conspirators, including Guy Fawkes, intended to blow up the House of Parliament, together with members of both Chambers and the King.—*Ed.*

when he was a baby. She entered the service of my grandmother von Westphalen when she was a girl of 8 or 9 and grew up with Moor, Mother and Edgar von Westphalen. She always had a great affection for the old von Westphalen. So did Moor. He never tired of telling us of the old Baron von Westphalen and his surprising knowledge of Shakespeare and Homer. The baron could recite some of Homer's songs by heart from beginning to end and he knew most of Shakespeare's dramas by heart in both German and English. In contrast to him, Moor's father—for whom Moor had great admiration—was a real eighteenth century 'Frenchman'. He knew Voltaire and Rousseau by heart just as the old Westphalen did Homer and Shakespeare. Moor's astonishing versatility was due without doubt to these 'hereditary' influences.

"To come back to Lenchen, I cannot say whether she came to my parents before or after they went to Paris (which was soon after their marriage). All I know is that Grandmother sent the girl to Mother 'as the best she could send, the faithful and loving Lenchen'. And the faithful and loving Lenchen remained with my parents and later her younger sister Marianne joined her. You will hardly remember this, for it was after your time. . . ."

17
Marx's Grave

It should really be called the Marx family grave. It is in Highgate Cemetery in the north of London on a hill overlooking the immense city. . . .

We Social-Democrats know no saints or tombs of saints. But millions of people remember with gratitude and respect the man who lies in that North London cemetery. And in thousands of years, when the coarseness and narrow-mindedness that try to restrain the working class's aspiration for freedom are but unbelievable legends of the past, free and noble men will stand at that grave with uncovered head and say to their attentive children: "Here lies Karl Marx."

Here lies Karl Marx and his family. A plain ivy-clad

marble stone lies pillow-like at the head of the marble-set grave. The stone bears the inscription:

Not all the members of the Marx family who have passed away are buried in the family grave. The three children who died in London were buried in other London cemeteries: Edgar (Mush) certainly, the two others probably in Whitefield Chapel churchyard, Tottenham Court Road. Jenny Marx, the favourite daughter, was laid to rest at Argenteuil, near Paris, where death snatched her from her flourishing family.

But although not all the children and grandchildren were given a place in the family grave, one who belongs to the family, though not by ties of blood, "Faithful Lenchen", Hélène Demuth, lies there.

Mrs. Marx and afterwards Marx had already decided that she should be buried in the family grave. And Engels, an Eckart as faithful as the faithful Lenchen, and the children who were still alive, together carried out the duty that he would have fulfilled by his own inclination.

The letters written by Marx's youngest daughter and published elsewhere show what Marx's children thought of Lenchen, what affection they had for her and how piously they honoured her memory.

On my return from my last visit to London, I passed through Paris and went to Draveil, where Lafargue and his wife Laura Marx have a pretty little country-house. There "Lörchen" and I indulged in memories of London and I spoke of my intention of writing this little book. Laura said to me exactly what Tussy said in the letter just quoted and repeated later orally: "Do not forget Lenchen!"

Well, I have not forgotten Lenchen and will not forget her. For she was a friend to me for forty years. And often enough in the London emigration period she was my "Providence" too. How often she helped me out with a sixpence when my purse was flat and things were not too bad with the Marxes—for if they were Lenchen had nothing to give. How often, when my skill as a tailor was not up to the mark, did she make some indispensable article of clothing that my financial condition offered no prospects of replacing last a few weeks longer.

When I first saw Lenchen she was 27 years old. She was not a beauty but she was pretty and had a good figure and her features were pleasant and attractive. She had suitors enough and several times she could have made a good match. But although she had not undertaken any obligation, her devoted heart found it quite natural that she should stay by Moor, Mrs. Marx and the children.

She remained, and the years of her youth slid by. She remained through need and hardships, through joys and sorrows. Rest did not come for her until death had mowed down those with whom she had thrown in her fate. She found rest at Engels' and it was there that she died, forgetful of herself to the end. Now she lies in the family grave.

* * *

Our friend Motteler, the "red postmaster", who now lives in Hampstead, not far from Highgate, gives the following description of the tomb:

"Marx's grave is set in white marble: the slab with the names and dates inscribed in black is of the same stone.

Some turf, the wild ivy I once brought from Switzerland, a few small rose-trees and grass sprouting between the gravel usual on graves here—that is all the modest decoration of the grave. I generally go past Highgate Cemetery, twice a week; I clear away the grass if it is too thick. Sometimes a little watering is necessary if the summer is like the last two (this year, although it is so rainy on the continent, there is a drought in England the like of which no one can remember and the grass is completely withered even in the parks). Even with Lessner's help I was unable to protect the grave against the ravages of the heat, so we were obliged to get the cemetery gardener to see to it regularly. This we did with the consent of the Avelings, who can only rarely go there because of the great distance at which they live."

18

Seeking Out Places of Old

When I went to England in May this year[1] I decided that after I had fulfilled my duties as an agitator and before returning I would go to the part of the city where we had lived as emigrants and especially to see the places where the Marx family had lived.

On June 8, a Monday, Tussy Marx, Aveling her husband and I set out from Sydenham to go to the corner of Tottenham Court Road, by Soho Square, by railway, cab and omnibus. From there we started our search. We went about it methodically.... Our wish was to "excavate" the London of the emigrants from the end of the forties to the fifties and sixties.

So there we were, at the corner of Tottenham Court Road, quite near Soho Square and Leicester Square, where the German and French emigrants had flocked together, driven by a feeling of solidarity in their destitution.

We first went to Soho Square. Nothing was changed. The same houses with the same coating of soot. Even some of the names of firms on the name plates were the same as of old.... It was like a dream. My youth was conjured up

---

[1] 1896.—*Ed*.

before my eyes, 40 or 45 years cleared away like a mist, blown away by the wind, and I saw myself, 25-year-old emigrant, crossing the square and going up a well-known side street towards Old Compton Street. The old model lodging-house in which we led such a jolly and yet desperate life a generation and a half ago was still there. I almost expected to see Red Wolff steal past or Conrad Schramm standing there. It was as if I had only left the day before.

How wonderful it is that in the ocean of houses in London there are streets and districts over which time passes unnoticed, which are unscathed by the tossing waves!...

On we went. Straight on, up to Church Street. Yes, there is the church, still as it was, and opposite it the inevitable pub, which has not changed either.... And those three-storey houses with two front windows, they too are just as we knew them. So is No. 14, where I lived eight years.

We go back and turn a corner. There is Macclesfield Street. Where is No. 6?... This must be where it was. But we look for it in vain. A new street has been laid out, the house in which Engels lived at the beginning of the emigration in London until he was sent by his strict father to the family business in Manchester has been swallowed up by the new street....

On we go. Here is Dean Street. Where is the house in which Marx and his family lived for years? I looked for it once before but could not find it. Later Engels told me the numbers had been changed. Here it is as hard to tell one house from another as to see a difference between two eggs, and I had never had time for longer searches in my previous visits to London. Lenchen, to whom I spoke about this shortly before her death, was also unable to say for certain which house it was. And Tussy, who was only a year old when the family moved from Dean Street to Kentish Town, could not, of course, remember it.

We had to proceed methodically. Very little had been changed in the street. We hesitated between several houses on the right from the Old Compton Street end. The only certain landmark that I could remember was a theatre on the other side near Old Compton Street. It had formerly belonged to a certain Miss Kelly but it had been rebuilt. It is now called Royalty Theatre and is much larger and broader than it was. As I did not know whether it had been enlarged to the left or the right I was not quite sure of the place of the only landmark I knew. Finally I decided that the choice must be between two houses. The outer appearance was no longer enough, I had to see the inside. The door of one of the houses was open. I went in, the staircase seemed familiar to me, and the whole outlay, as far as I could make it out from the entrance, corresponded to what I remembered. But most of the London houses are built to a standard, in series, and lack all individuality and originality. I went up to the first floor, but there I could not recognise anything, nothing seemed familiar to me.

Meanwhile, Marx's daughter and her husband had made further observations in the street. I told them the doubtful result of my investigations.

Must I go into the house next door? It was No. 28. If I was not mistaken that had been the number of Marx's house. Yes, it just occurred to me that at the beginning of my stay in London I had committed the number to my memory by a mnemotechnic trick—it was just double the number of my own house. So Engels must have been mistaken when he said that the numbers had been changed. Was it just a supposition on his part?

We rang the bell. A young woman opened the door. We asked her if she remembered the former owners and tenants.

"Yes, but only for the last nine years."

"Might I go in and see the house?"

"Certainly!" And she showed me up herself.

The staircase was as I remembered. The whole lay-out was too, and as we went on everything seemed more familiar to me. The stairs to the back room. Yes, it was all as I knew it.

Unfortunately, the rooms on the second floor, where Marx had lived, were locked. But as far as I could remember, everything was right, down to the last detail. My doubts disappeared one by one until at last I had the certainty: this was the house where Marx had lived.

As I came down I called out: "I've found it! This is it!"

Yes, that was the house that I had been in thousands of times, the house where Marx, assailed, tortured and worn out by the misery of emigration and the furious hatred of enemies without any conscience who shrank from no calumny, wrote his *Eighteenth Brumaire*, his *Herr Vogt* and his articles for the *New York Tribune*, which have now been collected under the title *Revolution and Counter-Revolution*, and where he did the enormous preparatory work for *Capital*....

Before leaving the house in Dean Street I wish to mention that when Marx arrived in London at the end of 1849 he at first lived in Camberwell.... There was unpleasantness there as a result of the landlord's bankruptcy, the creditors seizing the tenants' furniture according to English law. In May 1850—about the time I arrived in London—after a short stay in a family hotel near Leicester Square the Marx family moved to Dean Street. They stayed there for about seven years, after which they moved to Kentish Town, a part of London that was then still relatively rural.

There was nothing more for us to look for in Dean Street, so we went back to the corner of Tottenham Court Road and took an omnibus to Kentish Town.

There had not been much change in Tottenham Court Road. The appearance of the street was much the same as it had been, many of the old shops and firms still being there. The Whitefield Chapel or "Tabernacle" on the left was unchanged, only the churchyard had been closed. There poor "Mush" lies buried, and, if I am not mistaken, the two other children who died at an early age.

We approached Kentish Town.... The public-house there seemed familiar to me. True enough it was the old "Red Riding-Hood"....

We went that far by bus and then alighted and turned off into Maldon Road. How I felt at home there! But not for long! Soon I saw streets that did not exist when I left London. What was formerly partly fields is now built up.

Suddenly Tussy pointed to a house which was rather large for the London suburbs. "That's it!"

Yes, that was it, the house, or more correctly the cottage in Grafton Terrace in which Marx lived until ten years before his death. There was the small balcony from which Mrs. Marx, recuperating from a pock disease, used to talk to her three little daughters, who were living with me while she was ill. At first she could only whisper, but how she beamed when I brought the children along! The cottage was then No. 9, now it is No. 46.[1]

Not far off is 41, Maitland Park Road.... It was there that Marx died. The family moved into it in 1872 or 1873 when their first house became too large after the two eldest daughters got married.[2]

We went on in silence to Hampstead Heath where so much has changed and yet the former appearance is not completely lost. We looked for the places of old and finally had a snack in Jack Straw's Castle to give us strength for the long and tedious return journey.

Jack Straw's Castle. How often we had been there in days of old! In the very room in which we sat I had sat dozens of times with Marx, Mrs. Marx, the children, Lenchen and others.

That was a long time ago....

---

[1] Tussy maintains that at the very beginning, or at least when the Marx family lived in it, this house was No. 1. I think she is mistaken. In any case, the truth will soon be found out. (*Note by Liebknecht.—Ed.*)

[2] Marx lived at 9, Grafton Terrace from October 1856 to April 1864. From April 1864 to March 1875 he lived at 1, Modena Villas, Maitland Park Road. He lived at 41, Maitland Park Road from March 1875 to the time of his death.—*Ed.*

Wilhelm Liebknecht

REMINISCENCES OF ENGELS[1]

Frederick Engels had a clear bright head, free from any romantic or sentimental haze, that did not see men and things through coloured glasses or a misty atmosphere but always in clear bright air, saw brightly and clearly, with clear bright eyes, not remaining on the surface but seeing to the bottom of things, piercing them through and through. Those clear bright eyes, that *clairvoyance* in the true and healthy sense of the word, that perspicacity that Mother Nature gives but few people at birth, was an essential feature of Engels and I was immediately struck by it when we met for the first time....

It was late in summer 1849 by the blue Lake of Geneva, where we had set up several emigrant colonies after the failure of the Reich Constitution campaign.... Before that I had the opportunity of personally making the acquaintance of a number of "great men" of all kinds like Ruge, Heinzen, Julius Fröbel, Struve and various other leaders of the people in the Baden and Saxony "revolutions", but the closer my acquaintance with them became the more their halo faded and the smaller they seemed to me.

The more hazy the air, the bigger men and things seem. Frederick Engels had the quality that made the haze disappear before his clear-sighted eyes and men and things look like men and things are.

That piercing glance and the penetrating judgment result-

---

[1] Published in 1897.—*Ed.*

ing from it made me uncomfortable at first, and occasionally even hurt me. It was true that I had not been better impressed by the heroes of the Reich Constitution campaign than Engels, but I thought he underestimated the whole movement, which contained many valuable forces and much self-sacrificing enthusiasm. At the same time, the remains of "South-German placidity"—although I do not come from Southern Germany—that I still had at the time and that was thoroughly knocked out of me later in England, did not prevent us from agreeing in our general opinion of persons and things, although not always immediately. Neither was I long in noting that Engels, whose book on the British working-class movement I had read long before, and whose wealth and variety of knowledge personal association with him had taught me to admire, always had solid and definite grounds for his opinion. I looked up to him, he had already achieved much and was five years older than me—the equivalent of a whole century at that age.

I soon noticed, too, that he was efficient in military matters. In the course of the conversation I learned that the articles that the *Neue Rheinische Zeitung* had published on the revolutionary war in Hungary and that were attributed to a high-ranking officer in the Hungarian army because they always proved to be correct, were written by Engels. And yet, as he himself told me, laughing, he had no other material than all the other newspapers had. This came almost exclusively from the Austrian Government, which lied in the most brazen-faced way. It did the same with Hungary as the Spanish Government now with Cuba[1] —it always won. But Engels here made use of his *clairvoyance*. He took no heed of phrase-mongering. He already had Röntgen's X-rays in his head, and they, as we know, suffer no refraction and do not make a U out of an X; by means of them he saw through what was unessential for the establishment of the truth and did not allow any haze or mirage to lead him astray but stuck to what was substantial—to facts. No matter with what scorn of death the Austrian Government issued its Münchhausen proclamations it had to mention certain facts: the names of the places

---

[1] The allusion is to the failure of the Spanish Government to suppress the popular rising which flared up in 1895 on the Island of Cuba, then a Spanish colony.—*Ed*.

where the clashes took place, where the troops were at the beginning and at the end of the battle, the time of the clashes, the troop movements, etc. And out of these tiny bits and pieces "unser Fritz" with his clear bright eyes put together like Cuvier the real picture of the events in the fighting area. With a good map of the theatre of operations one could conclude with mathematical accuracy from the dates and places that the victorious Austrians were being pushed farther and farther back while the defeated Hungarians continued to go farther and farther forward. The calculation was so correct, too, that the day after the Austrian army had inflicted a decisive defeat on the Hungarians on paper it was thrown out of Hungary in complete disarray....

Engels, by the way, seemed born to be a soldier: he had clear sight, quickness of perception and appreciation of the smallest circumstance, rapid decision and imperturbable coolness. Later he wrote a number of excellent essays on military questions and, though incognito, gained recognition by first-class military experts who had no idea that the anonymous author of the pamphlets was one of the most notorious rebels....

In London we jokingly called him the General, and if there had been another revolution in his lifetime we would have had in Engels our Carnot,[1] the organiser of armies and victories, the military brain....

After a short stay in Switzerland with Engels I met him in the following year in London whither he had at first proceeded. After that I was in constant touch with him. He did actually leave London, where I lived, in 1850 for his father's business in Manchester, for like other Rhine manufacturers, his father had an English branch office; but he paid us frequent visits, sometimes rather long ones, in London. He also wrote almost daily to Marx, who regularly communicated as much of his letters as was not strictly private to us, i.e., the more trusted members of the frequently changing "Marx clique". It is true that I never had such close relations with Engels as with Marx, in whose

---

[1] *Carnot, Lazare Nicolas* (1753-1823)—French political and military figure in the period of the French bourgeois revolution at the end of the eighteenth century.—*Ed.*

house I was an almost daily guest, almost a member of his family, for twelve years.

Marx's death brought me nearer to Engels, who now had the double task of replacing Marx and of executing his will.

Only now did he, who so far, to use his own words, had been second fiddle, show all he was capable of. He showed that he could play first fiddle too. The energy that he had been obliged for a score of years to devote mostly to business now went entirely to that double task. He completed *Capital*, as far as was possible, developed astonishing activity in scientific work of his own and owing to his extraordinary capacity for work still found time for a voluminous international correspondence. And Engels' letters were often treatises, guides and directions in politics and economics.

He helped everywhere he was needed; he stirred up all around him. As adviser, exhorter, warner, he took part until shortly before his death like an active soldier in the battles of the great international working-class movement which was carrying out the motto that he and his friend Marx, scenting the morning breeze of the February Revolution, had proclaimed to the workers at the beginning of 1848:

Proletarians of all countries, unite!

They have united.

And no power in the world can bar the road to the united proletariat of the world.

On November 28, 1890, we celebrated Engels' seventieth birthday in London. He was as fresh, witty and ready for the fight as ever in his merriest, warmest youth. And when three years later he called out to the Berlin workers in Konkordia Hall[1]: "Comrades, I am convinced that you will do your duty in the future too!" there was not one among the thousands listening to him with enthusiasm and contemplating him with love and gratitude who did not ask in astonishment, "Can that young man be 73 already?"

Not quite two years later, on August 6, 1895, on my re-

---

[1] Engels made a speech at a Social-Democrat meeting in Berlin on September 22, 1893.—*Ed.*

turn from the big trade union festival in Bremen, I found the sad telegram on my desk in the editorial office of *Vorwärts*:

"General died yesterday night 10.30. No struggle, unconscious since noon. Please inform Soldat, Singer."

"Soldat" (soldier) meant me.

Since the spring we, that is three persons in Germany,[1] had known that the "General" was suffering from an incurable cancerous infection of the throat. But although the stroke was not unexpected, it was a hard one, a terrible one.

So he was laid low, that titanic mind who together with Marx laid the foundations of scientific socialism and taught the tactics of socialism, who at the early age of 24 wrote the classical work *The Condition of the Working Class in England*, the co-author of the *Communist Manifesto*, Karl Marx's *alter ego* who helped him to call to life the International Working Men's Association, the author of *Anti-Dühring*, that encyclopaedia of science of crystal transparency accessible to anybody who can think, the author of *The Origin of the Family* and so many other works, essays and newspaper articles, the friend, the adviser, the leader and the fighter—he was dead.

But his spirit lives wherever class-conscious proletarians live and fight.

---

[1] Wilhelm Liebknecht, August Bebel and Paul Singer.—*Ed.*

Friedrich Lessner

BEFORE 1848 AND AFTER[1]

(Reminiscences of an Old Communist)

1

During the storms of the latter half of the forties I was already a Communist, a passionate fighter for social ownership of the means of production and for brotherly co-operation between men....

When, as a young tailor's journeyman, I heard a communist speech for the first time in Hamburg in 1846 and then read Weitling's *Guarantees of Harmony and Freedom* I thought communism would be a reality in a couple of years.... But when I heard Karl Marx in 1847 and read and understood the *Communist Manifesto* it was clear to me that the enthusiasm and good-will of individuals are not enough to effect a transformation of human society.... What I lost in enthusiasm and fancy I gained in consciousness of the aim and knowledge....

In the workshop in which I found employment I made friends with a few colleagues who had already worked in Switzerland, Paris and London. There they had become acquainted with communist ideas....

* * *

There was at that time in Hamburg a Workers' Educational Society which was the meeting-place of all progressive workers. They met every evening to read the newspapers, hold discussions or sing and learn foreign languages. Most

---

[1] Published in 1898.—*Ed.*

of the newspapers were of oppositional trend; the discussions centred mainly on questions of communism and the songs that the song section favoured were radical freedom songs....

In the Workers' Educational Society Wilhelm Weitling was considered as the man of the future. The respect he enjoyed in our circles was boundless. He was the idol of his followers.

I was introduced to the Workers' Educational Society by my colleagues in November 1846 and was soon admitted as a member. From then on I attended the discussion evenings regularly....

One of my colleagues gave me Wilhelm Weitling's *Guarantees of Harmony and Freedom* to read. This book was then much read among workers. It passed from one to another, for few had their own copy. I read it once, twice, three times. It was then that it first occurred to me that the world could be different from what it was....

That period, during which the discussions at the Workers' Educational Society and Weitling's *Guarantees* revolutionised my views and considerably widened my horizon, was decisive for my political opinions....

When, on April 1, 1847, instead of going to the barracks in Weimar, I boarded a ship that was to take me to England, I felt as though I had left my past behind me on the continent to begin a new life in England—a life that I made up my mind to devote to the fight for the emancipation of mankind.

* * *

When I had decided to go to London, Martens[1] gave me a recommendation for the London Workers' Educational Society in which I was given a friendly welcome.

The London Workers' Educational Society was founded on February 7, 1840....

After a few days I managed to find work and then I regularly attended the Society of which I was a member. I was also admitted to the League of the Just, which precisely at that time was changed to the Communist League.

---

[1] *Martens, Joahim*—one of the leaders of the Workers' Educational Society in Hamburg and the Hamburg community of the Communist League.—*Ed*.

The influence of Weitling continued to decline in London, while the names of Marx and Engels came to the fore.

2

So far I did not know these two men. I only knew that they lived in Brussels, where they edited the *Deutsche-Brüsseler Zeitung*. I then had no idea that the appearance of these men would be the beginning of a new era in the history of socialism....

A few months after my arrival in London—in the summer of 1847—the First Congress of the League took place. Engels and Wilhelm Wolff came to it, but Marx was not present. The Congress reorganised the League. "What remained of the old mystical name of the time of conspiracy was done away with," said Engels. "Henceforth it was called the Communist League."...

In summer 1847, Étienne Cabet, the famous author of *Voyage en Icarie*, published an appeal to the French Communists in which he said: "As we here (in France) are persecuted, calumniated and slandered by the government, the priests, the bourgeoisie and even the revolutionary Republicans, as attempts are even made to deprive us of our existence, to ruin us physically and morally, let us leave France and go to Icaria to found a Communist colony there." Cabet then expressed the hope that about 20-30 thousand Communists would be found to carry out that plan.

This appeal was also addressed to the London Workers' Educational Society. About September 1847 Cabet himself came to London to win us over to his idea. The discussion of his proposal lasted a whole week. In the end the Society decided against all experiments. We answered that we could not decide to follow Cabet because in our opinion he was taking the wrong path. We respected Cabet personally but opposed his emigration plan.... Every fighter for justice and truth must consider it his duty to remain in the country, to enlighten the people and to inspire new courage in those who were drooping, to lay the foundation for a new organisation of society and to offer keen resistance to rascals. If upright men, fighters for a better future went away and left the field to the ignorant and the rascals, the whole of Europe would necessarily be doomed....

Those were the main grounds on which we considered Cabet's proposal as fatal and called to Communists in all countries: "Brothers, let us stand in the breach here in old Europe; let us act and fight, for only here will the conditions for the foundation of common ownership be to hand, here or nowhere will it first be established."

That was our rejection of Cabet's proposal.... It showed that Communists who reflected, who were already under the influence of Marx and Engels, condemned all utopian attempts even at that early period....

Cabet left London. Soon afterwards, at the end of November 1847, the Second Congress of the Communist League met, and Karl Marx was present. He and Engels came from Brussels to expound at the Congress the principles of modern socialism. The Congress lasted ten days.

Only delegates attended the sittings, and I was not one of them. But we others knew what it was all about and waited with no little suspense for the results of the discussion. We soon heard that the Congress had unanimously declared for the principles expounded by Marx and Engels and had charged them with writing a Manifesto. When at the beginning of 1848 the manuscript of the *Communist Manifesto* arrived from Brussels I was to play a modest part in the publication of this epoch-making document: I delivered the manuscript to the printer and took the proofsheets from him to Karl Schapper for checking.

About this time I saw Marx and Engels for the first time. I shall never forget the impression they made upon me.

Marx was then still a young man, about 28 years old, but he greatly impressed us all. He was of medium height, broad-shouldered, powerful in build and energetic in his deportment. His brow was high and finely shaped, his hair thick and pitch-black, his gaze piercing. His mouth already had the sarcastic line that his opponents feared so much. Marx was a born leader of the people. His speech was brief, convincing and compelling in its logic. He never said a superfluous word; every sentence was a thought and every thought was a necessary link in the chain of his demonstration. Marx had nothing of the dreamer about him. The more I realised the difference between the communism of Weitling's time and that of the *Communist Manifesto*, the more clearly I saw that Marx represented the manhood of socialist thought.

Frederick Engels, Marx's spiritual brother, was more of the Germanic type. Slim, agile, with fair hair and moustache, he was more like a smart young lieutenant of the guard than a scholar.

Although Engels always stressed the importance of his immortal friend, he himself had an enormous share in the founding and spreading of modern socialism. He was a man you respected and loved once you knew him intimately....

* * *

We in the Workers' Educational Society were in a certain state of excitement at that time. We firmly believed that it must "start" soon and we still had no idea how much education and organisation work had yet to be done to make the proletariat capable of shattering the bourgeois world.

The *Communist Manifesto* left the press in February 1848. We received it at the same time as the news of the outbreak of the February Revolution in Paris.

I cannot render the powerful impression that this news produced upon us. We were intoxicated with enthusiasm. Only one feeling, one thought filled us: to stake our life and all we had for the liberation of mankind!

The London Central Committee of the League immediately delegated its powers to the leading body in Brussels, which in its turn delegated them to Marx and Engels, empowering them to constitute a new Central Authority in Paris.

Immediately after this decision Marx was arrested in Brussels and compelled to leave for France, which was precisely where he intended to go.

3

The Paris events deeply impressed the working class in England. The Chartist movement, which had occupied the minds of the English proletariat since the middle of the thirties, received a new impulse from the victorious course of the February Revolution. The very outbreak of that revolution was welcomed by the London workers with a big

June days in Paris in 1848

Uprising of the Paris proletariat in June 1848

Communards fighting in Père-la-Chaise cemetery

Communards' last battle

demonstration. The members of the Communist League took part in the demonstration just as they had supported the Chartist movement by all means at their disposal.

Ernest Jones, the most popular and efficient leader of the Chartists, occasionally visited our Society, where I had the opportunity to get to know that courageous and self-sacrificing agitator. Jones was small but well-knit.... He could both write and speak German and he was one of the few Chartists who at the same time understood and preached socialism.

On March 13 there was a meeting on Kensington Common in London. Jones spoke at it. He called on the people not to fear the pitiful men of the law, the police, the soldiers or the shopkeepers sworn in as special constables who ran away from a couple of street urchins. "Down with the ministry! Dissolve Parliament! The Charter and no capitulation!"

At the beginning of April a Chartist Covenant was formed in London which was to show more energy in support of the Petition that had so far been sent to Parliament every year for the introduction of the political freedoms demanded by the workers. The Petition was to be handed in on April 10, not as formerly by a few delegates, but by the masses of the workers themselves. It was intended to impress on Parliament the determination of the proletariat to put its demands into effect by force if necessary.

London offered a curious sight on the morning of April 10. All factories and shops were closed. The London bourgeois were armed to maintain "order". Among them was Napoleon the Little, later the burgher of Wilhelmshöhe.[1]

The members of the Communist League had decided to take part in the demonstration. We armed ourselves with all sorts of weapons. I can still quite well remember the comical impression made on me by Georg Eccarius[2] when he showed me a big pair of tailor's scissors, sharpened till they glistened, with which he intended to defend himself against the attacks of the constables.

---

[1] *Wilhelmshöhe*—a castle near Kassel (Hesse-Nassau) where Louis Napoleon was held captive by the Prussian Government after the defeat of his army at Sedan (1870).—*Ed.*

[2] *Eccarius, Georg* (1818-1889)—German tailor, member of the Communist League and the General Council of the First International, was close to Marx and Engels.—*Ed.*

The workers assembled on Kensington Common to join the procession to Parliament. But suddenly we heard that Feargus O'Connor, the leader of the demonstration, was against a mass procession because the Government was ready to oppose it with armed force.... Many followed O'Connor's advice, others pushed forward, and as a result there were bloody clashes between the police and the Chartists. As O'Connor's attempts at appeasement had destroyed the unity of the demonstrators, success could no longer be counted upon.... Bitterly disappointed, we left the scene of the demonstration, where we had assembled so full of expectation an hour earlier.

* * *

At the same time as these stormy events in West Europe, the revolution broke out in Central Europe. This particularly aroused us. The discussions at the Workers' Educational Society's evenings became more and more excited and heated. Everybody was ready to hurry to the battle-fields in Germany, but most of us had not the means to carry out this intention immediately. It was not until July 1848 that I had saved up enough to be able to undertake the journey to Germany.

During these preparations we received the discomforting news of the terrible defeat of the June Revolution. Its effect upon us cannot be expressed in words. I can still vividly remember that I read a good twenty times the article that Marx wrote about this event in the *Neue Rheinische Zeitung* (June 29, 1848), for it was the best expression of what we felt.

4

I arrived in Cologne at midsummer 1848. This city had a special attraction for me because of the men who were serving the revolution there—Marx, Engels, Wilhelm Wolff, Freiligrath,[1] Schapper and Moll were then in Cologne where the *Neue Rheinische Zeitung* was published.

The first thing I did was to look for work so as to be able to remain in Cologne....

---

[1] *Freiligrath, Ferdinand* (1810-1876)—German revolutionary poet, one of the editors of the *Neue Rheinische Zeitung.—Ed.*

When I had got work I joined the Workers' Society, the leaders of which were Dr. Gottschalk, Lieutenant Anneke, Schapper, Moll, Nothjung and D'Ester. Besides this there was also a Democratic Society[1] frequented by Wilhelm Wolff, Marx, Freiligrath and others. There I got to know Wilhelm Wolff, who often gave talks on current political events. It was a real pleasure to hear that man speak. His vigorous, humorous way of giving a "political survey" was admired by everybody; he could group even the better known and less exciting events so skilfully and deal with a matter seriously or satirically according to its nature. Occasionally Freiligrath also came and later I made friends with him....

In November 1848, there was a meeting of the Democratic Society at which Marx broke the news that Robert Blum had been shot by sentence of a field court-martial in Vienna. The meeting was in full swing when Marx appeared. Silence immediately fell over the hall. Marx went up to the rostrum and read out the despatch from Vienna on Blum's death. We were horrified. Then a storm seemed to blow through the hall. I thought the German people would now rise like one man to fight the revolution to the end. I and the others were mistaken. It happened quite differently. The Bürgermeisters kissed the hands of the tyrants who had had the noblest sons of the people murdered.

* * *

The intensification of reaction was manifested above all by persecution of the opposition press, particularly the *Neue Rheinische Zeitung*, which was inflexible and fearless in the defence of freedom and justice. On February 7, 1849, the first lawsuit against the editors of the *Neue Rheinische Zeitung* took place, followed on the next day by the second and finally, on May 18, 1849, the paper was completely suppressed. The last issue appeared in red type....

Marx did not defend himself, he accused the ministry. Karl Marx, editor-in-chief, and Frederick Engels were charged with "insulting in an article printed in the *Neue*

---

[1] The *Democratic Society* was founded in Cologne in spring 1848. Its members were petty-bourgeois democrats, craftsmen and workers. Marx, Engels and their supporters joined it in order to influence its members, especially the proletarian elements.—*Ed*.

Rheinische Zeitung the Chief Procurator and the gendarmes in the discharge of their duties". The court was crowded. When the State Procurator and the attorneys had spoken Marx made a speech. He spoke for about an hour, his legal arguments ringing calm, dignified and energetic, attacking with ever-increasing force the State Procurator, the old bureaucracy, the old army, the old courts, the old judges who were born and educated and had grown old in the service of absolutism. "The first duty of the press," Marx said, "is now to *undermine all the foundations of the existing political system.*"

After a few months Marx was expelled from Prussia, Engels went to Baden ... while those who remained in Cologne extended their agitation to the countryside, for we already understood the importance of agitation among the peasants. (When I attended the Cologne Party Congress in 1893 I was invited by some peasants to Worringen, near Cologne. They still remembered me from 1848 and 1849.)

Our spare time was spent in making cartridges which were sent to Baden. They were naturally made in secret. Red Becker[1] procured the shot and powder and each did what he could to promote the revolution....

5

Counter-revolution was victorious all along the line.... The Communist League was revived and took steps to organise the party of the proletariat in secret. As all kinds of doubtful elements had made their way into the League in London the Central Committee was transferred to Cologne on Marx's proposal. My task in Mainz was to revive the local organisation of the League and to win the workers over to our aims. Outwardly our propaganda consisted only in spreading leaflets. We were so well organised that we could flood Mainz with leaflets within an hour. The police did not succeed once in catching the "culprits".

In October 1850, the Frankfort comrades gave me the assignment of reorganising the League in Nuremberg, which I succeeded in doing. Unfortunately our agitation did not

---

[1] Nickname for *Hermann Becker* (1820-1885)—German publicist, member of the Communist League.—*Ed.*

go on for long.... The police official was the hero of the day. Reaction did not shrink from any means capable of suppressing the freedom movement.

In June 1851 I too was arrested in Mainz.

* * *

On October 4, 1852, I appeared before the Cologne jury.... The case lasted more than five weeks. I shall not enter into details of the trial here, for they were given by Marx in his *Revelations about the Cologne Communist Trial*....

The sentence was a heavy blow for me. I had to serve three years' detention in a fort....

The four and a half years in prison seemed to me a terrible nightmare.... On January 27, 1856, I was released. "Free!" as if Germany then had not been a vast prison! That was the impression I immediately got when, after a visit to relatives of my fellow-prisoners in Breslau, Erfurt and Freiburg, I arrived in Weimar. Here I tried to do some agitation, but the people were so terrified that they shrank at the very word "communism".

I myself was homeless. The authorities to whom I applied for a travel permit would not recognise me, a disreputable Communist, as one of their countrymen. Only after going from one to another many times and great insistence did I manage to get some papers. Then I went to London via Hamburg....

6

In May 1856 I arrived in London. Soon afterwards I paid a visit to Freiligrath ... and then went to see Karl Marx, who presented me with the works of his so far published to replace my collection of books which had been confiscated. I also sought out my old friends of 1848, Karl Pfänder, Georg Eccarius and others. Here I also made acquaintance with German emigrants, of whom many were staying in London, Wilhelm Liebknecht among them. When I had found work I again attended the Communist Workers' Educational Society which was then in a very sorry plight. The reason for this was the following: after the collapse of the revolutionary movement of 1848 many members had left the Society and the remaining ones had gradually turned petty bourgeois. There was no longer any trace of communist views in the Society, which had become through and through spiritless, exactly to the liking of our liberals....

This situation in the Communist Workers' Educational Society grieved me. I began to study the members and make friends with some of them. After I had succeeded in this we began our spade-work.... Wilhelm Liebknecht began attending the Society again and so did Marx, who delivered a series of lectures on political economy without accepting any compensation, for he never accepted a penny from the workers in his whole life. The membership increased....

From 1860 to 1864 I spent my time extending my knowledge. I regularly attended lectures at London University by Professors Huxley, Tyndall and Hofmann on physiology, geology and chemistry. These eminent scientists' lectures were much attended by the German workers generally. Here again it was Karl Marx who urged us to do so and he himself occasionally attended them.

* * *

In 1864 the old disintegrated Communist League celebrated its rebirth, although in another form. The International Working Men's Association was founded. Socialism began to occupy the workers again, and more intensely than ever. The fruits of our former activity were maturing....

After the Commune difficult times set in for the International. The British press, which controlled public opinion, calumniated and vilified us. A state was reached when we could not get premises in London for our meetings. When we wanted to celebrate the first anniversary of the Commune on March 18, 1872, we found the hall we had rented cordoned off. Then I arranged for a special house, in which we held the sittings of the General Council, to be rented....

After 1870, the fight against the International from the outside continued to gain in intensity, and most governments took measures against its supporters. In France a special law was even passed and there were men in the

English trade unions who agitated against it. Besides this, there were Mikhail Bakunin's[1] filthy intrigues within the organisation. Marx's position at this time was no enviable one. He was overloaded with work for the International. He wrote all the manifestos, addresses and other material that was published for the International. Besides there was his very bulky correspondence and the great demand made on his time by the emigrant Communards who came to London. Marx satisfied all these claims without any compensation, although he had to struggle desperately for his own existence. His household expenses kept on increasing, especially after the Commune. In his house one could always meet a number of French emigrants who had to be accommodated and maintained. That was an especially difficult time for Mrs. Marx. She often came to my wife and myself for advice or to discuss some family trouble. But all that could not deter her from sincere and lively participation in the proletarian movement.

The struggle against Bakunin was to be fought out at the Hague Congress. Bakunin promised to be there and this decided Marx to go too in order to settle the dispute with him. The Hague Congress was the only congress of the International which Marx attended. In other cases he remained in London and left others the opportunity of distinguishing themselves at congresses. If he finally decided to go to the Hague it was only to put an end once for all to Bakunin's intrigues. Frederick Engels also went and Mrs. Marx and her children profited by the occasion to go there.

The Congress took place at the beginning of September 1872. There were 65 delegates present....

Mikhail Bakunin did not keep his word, he did not come to the Congress. But his creatures were there and played a miserable role. The Congress had mainly two questions to settle: 1) the transfer of the seat of the General Council, and 2) Bakunin's expulsion from the International. Frederick Engels spoke on the first point and favoured the transfer of the seat of the General Council to New York. His proposal was adopted. The expulsion of Bakunin took place at a closed

---

[1] *Bakunin, Mikhail Alexandrovich* (1814-1876)—Russian revolutionary, publicist, one of the ideologists of anarchism; resolutely opposed Marxism in the First International; expelled from the International for splitting activities.—*Ed.*

sitting: even the opponents of Marx condemned Bakunin's intrigues and voted for his expulsion....

While in The Hague, Marx was stormed by journalists from literally every civilised country: everybody wanted to see him and to know his opinion on the aims and desires of the International....

The 1872 Hague Congress was the last event of the old International....

7

About this time I made frequent visits to Marx's family. His house was open to every reliable comrade. I shall never forget the pleasant hours which, like many others, I spent among Marx's family. Mrs. Marx produced a particularly vivid impression. She was a tall, very beautiful woman, very distinguished and yet so good-natured, lovable, witty and so free from pride and stiffness that one felt as much at ease and at home in her presence as with one's own mother or sister.... As I have already said, she was full of enthusiasm for the working-class movement, and every success, no matter how small, against the bourgeoisie gave her the greatest satisfaction and pleasure.

Marx always attached particular importance to meetings and talks with workers. He considered it highly important to hear their opinion of the movement and sought the company of those who spoke frankly to him and spared him flattery. He was always ready to discuss the most important political and economic problems with them. He was quick in ascertaining whether they understood those questions well enough, and the more they did, the greater was his joy.

During the time of the International he never missed a sitting of the General Council. After the sittings Marx and most of us members of the Council generally went to a decent public-house for a glass of beer and a chat. On the way home Marx often spoke of the normal working-day in general and of the eight-hour day in particular. He often said, "We are fighting for the eight-hour working-day, but we frequently work more than twice as long...."

In fact, Marx unfortunately worked far too much. It is beyond the conception of outsiders how much labour power

Karl Marx. 1867

Jenny Marx

Laura, daughter of Marx

Karl Marx and his eldest daughter Jenny

and time the International alone cost him. And yet he had to work hard for his living and to study for hours in the British Museum to collect material for his works on history and economics. On his way home to Maitland Park Road, Haverstock Hill, in the north of London, he often dropped in to see me, for I lived not far from the Museum, to discuss some question concerning the International. When he got home he would have his meal, after which he rested for a while and then resumed his work. Often, too often, he worked late into the night or even the early hours of the morning, especially as his short evening rest was frequently cut short by visits from Party comrades.

Like all really great men, Marx was not at all conceited. He appreciated every honest striving and every opinion based on self-reliant thinking. As I have already said, he was always keen to hear the opinion of the most ordinary workers on the working-class movement. Thus he often came to me in the afternoon, took me with him on his walk, and spoke to me about all sorts of things. I naturally let him do as much of the talking as possible, for it was a real pleasure to hear him talk and develop his arguments. I was always fascinated by his conversation and found it hard to leave him. In general he was splendid company and exerted a powerful attraction and even fascination on all who came into contact with him. His wit was inexhaustible and his laughter came right from the heart. When our Party comrades managed to achieve a victory in any country he would express his joy in the most unconstrained way and rejoice noisily, his joy infecting all those around him.

From their early youth Marx's three daughters also took a most heartfelt interest in the working-class movement of the time, which was always the main topic in Marx's family. Relations between Marx and his daughters were the most intimate and unconstrained that one can imagine. The girls treated their father more as a brother or friend, for Marx scorned the exterior attributes of paternal authority. In serious matters he was his children's adviser, otherwise, according as his time allowed, their playmate.

Marx had an extreme liking for children generally.... Often, when he had nothing to do in town and went for a walk to Hampstead Heath, the author of *Capital* could be seen bustling about with a lot of children.

The death in 1883 of his eldest daughter, who had all the qualities of her mother—and she had only good ones—was a new blow to Marx at a time which was most difficult and fateful for him. Hardly twelve months earlier, on December 2, 1881, he had lost the faithful companion of his life. These were blows from which he never recovered.

Marx already had a nasty cough. When you heard it you thought his broad powerful figure would burst. This cough troubled him all the more as his constitution had been undermined by years of continuous overworking. In the middle of the seventies the doctors forbade him to smoke and as Marx was a heavy smoker, this was a terrible sacrifice. On my first visit to him after the doctors' order he was quite pleased and proud to be able to tell me that he had not smoked for so and so many days, and that he would not do so until the doctors allowed him to. On every subsequent visit he would tell me how long it was since he had given up smoking and that he had not smoked all that time. He did not seem able to believe himself that he would manage it. His pleasure was all the greater when some time later the doctor allowed him a cigar a day....

* * *

On March 15, 1883, I got a letter from Engels informing me of Marx's death. The news shattered me. Marx's trusted acquaintances knew what the working-class movement had lost. It had lost not only a man of great intelligence and vast learning, but a man of consistent, iron character. What an abundance of knowledge was laid with him in the grave was proved by the works he left behind him, although they did not contain a tenth of what he had intended to write. The proof of his heroic character is his whole life, rich in struggle and sacrifice.

Marx was firmly convinced that the working masses would sooner or later understand him and draw from his teachings the strength to overthrow bourgeois society and work with clear consciousness to build a new society.

Friedrich Lessner

A WORKER'S REMINISCENCES OF FREDERICK ENGELS[1]

May I, before I close my eyes for ever, bequeath my reminiscences of a long acquaintance and friendship with the great fighter Frederick Engels. Although much has been written and said about him since his death, I still think it justifiable to relate my experience of the association I had with him since 1847.

My account will, admittedly, not be so complete as I should wish. Half a century has passed since I made Engels' acquaintance and I must write everything from memory. My advanced age is an obstacle too, my hand is no longer as steady as I could wish it to be for writing; that is why I hope I shall be excused if my account is not so good as it should be.

1

My first acquaintance with Frederick Engels, and also with Karl Marx, dates from the interesting period at the end of 1847, in London. It was in the Communist Workers' Society, the only association of that time that still exists and still champions the working-class movement of today.[2] It was at the memorable meeting at which the international

---

[1] Published in 1901.—*Ed.*
[2] By the end of the 19th century the Society had degenerated into an ordinary club.—*Ed.*

working-class movement of today was founded. Marx, Engels and W. Wolff came with the Belgian comrade Tedesco to London in order to agree on the principles and the tactics of the new movement. Today the whole world knows that Marx and Engels were charged at that Communist Congress with composing a Communist Manifesto.

I had already heard of Marx and Engels before then, through the *Deutsche-Brüsseler Zeitung*, which appeared in 1847 and 1848. Engels' book *The Condition of the Working Class in England*, the first edition of which was published in 1845, was on sale in the Communist Workers' Society in London. That was the first book which I bought, and from it I got my first view of the working-class movement. The other book from which I learned at that time was Weitling's *Guarantees of Harmony and Freedom*.

The presence of Marx, Engels, W. Wolff and others in London produced a great impression not only on the members of the Communist Workers' Society, but also on those of the Communist League. Much was expected from this meeting and hopes were not frustrated but, on the contrary, greatly exceeded. The publication of the *Communist Manifesto*, which was the momentous outcome of this memorable meeting, is the factual proof of my statement.

Engels differed from Karl Marx in outward appearance. He was tall and slim, his movements were quick and vigorous, his manner of speaking brief and decisive, his carriage erect, giving a soldierly touch. He was of a very lively nature; his wit was to the point. Everybody who associated with him inevitably got the impression that he was dealing with a man of great intelligence....

With strangers Engels was reserved, more so in his later years. You had to know him well in order to form a correct opinion of him, just as he too gave a man his confidence only when he knew him thoroughly....

With him you could not pretend: he immediately saw whether he was being importuned with tales or told the truth without detour. Engels was a good judge of men, although he was mistaken in some cases....

Engels' portrait would be incomplete if the words of his old English friend George Julian Harney, the editor of the Chartist paper *The Northern Star*, who knew him since

1843, were not quoted. After Engels' death Harney wrote: "It was in 1843 that Engels came over from Bradford to Leeds and enquired for me at *The Northern Star* office. A tall handsome young man, with a countenance of almost boyish youthfulness, whose English, in spite of his German birth and education, was even then remarkable for its accuracy. He told me he was a constant reader of *The Northern Star* and took a keen interest in the Chartist movement. Thus began our friendship over 50 years ago."

In spite of all his work, Harney wrote, Engels always found time for his friends, and gave them advice and help when necessary. His vast learning and his influence never made him "stand-offish"; on the contrary, at 75 he was just as modest and ready to give credit for the work of others as at 22. He was extraordinarily hospitable, liked a joke, and his laugh was contagious. He was the soul of the conversation and had the knack of making his guests—he associated with Owenites, Chartists, trade-unionists and Socialists—feel at home and at ease.

2

My closer acquaintance with Engels and Marx dated back to Cologne, where I arrived from London at the end of June 1848. There I was introduced to the editorial board of the *Neue Rheinische Zeitung*.... Engels knew that I was a tailor and he named me his court tailor, but the only work I did for him was to restore and retouch his wardrobe. Neither Engels nor Marx attached much importance to dress and their money situation at the time was far from brilliant.

I was then quite young, and had never been in the habit of pushing myself to the fore. We therefore met mostly at popular meetings or on other occasions and greeted one another as battle comrades. Short as our association was, I learned at that time to appreciate the two rare men and I expected much from them in the future.

The *Communist Manifesto* left no room for doubt about the accuracy of their knowledge of the existing society, and the easily understandable way in which it was written brought the class antagonisms within the comprehension of the ordinary worker. But it was in the *Neue Rheinische*

Zeitung that Marx and Engels first really showed that besides knowledge they also had an indomitable will.

The black-and-white reaction[1] soon found out what superior opponents they were up against and did all in their power to get the *Neue Rheinische Zeitung* out of their way. Not succeeding in this, they resorted to still more drastic measures to suppress the paper. Two lawsuits were conducted, the first on February 7, the second on February 8, against the Rhine Committee of the Democrats. I attended both with great interest and it was a delight to see and hear with what great superiority the black-and-white reaction was opposed. Even these two men's opponents could not help admiring them!

After the suppression by force of the *Neue Rheinische Zeitung* and the illegal banning of Karl Marx, the members of the editorial board scattered in all directions. Marx went to Paris, Engels to Pfalz, where the movement for a Reich Constitution had flared up. . . .

3

After the defeat of the revolution in Baden Engels and many other fighters had to flee to Switzerland. Engels only stayed there for a short time and then went to London. There he found Marx and a large number of German emigrants.

Very hard times set in both for Engels and for Marx and his family in London, as neither had any means. Eleanor Marx told of those hard times in one of her many essays.

It was at that time that Marx, Engels, Liebknecht, Wilhelm Wolff and others took an active part in the Communist Educational Society, in which there were then many political emigrants of all trends. There were such divergencies over recent political events and over the future, and life in emigration was attended with so much unpleasantness that it was no wonder friction soon set in. . . .

As far as I remember, Engels must have left London in 1850 to take up work in a cotton mill in Manchester in which

---

[1] The Prussian counter-revolution: black and white were the colours of the Prussian flag.—*Ed.*

his father was a partner.... He left Manchester in 1870 to devote all his time to study and collaboration with Marx.

In Manchester Engels associated mainly with Wilhelm Wolff, Samuel Moore and Karl Schorlemmer. He occasionally came to London to see Marx, or else Marx went to Manchester. Visits were rare, however, and were not long, but correspondence was all the more lively....

In 1859 I wrote a letter to Engels, asking him incidentally for a photograph, which I received together with an excellent letter. I should have liked to quote the letter here, but in spite of much seeking I have not been able to find it.

In autumn 1870 Engels went to London with his wife and settled not far from Marx in the well-known house near Primrose Hill where he lived till shortly before his death.

The outbreak of the Franco-Prussian War (1870) aroused Engels' interest and consequently took up much of his time. His articles on the war in *Pall Mall Gazette* proved his knowledge of military matters and won him the nickname the "General". He foretold many of the defeats of the French army. While the German troops were concentrating around the French northern army, Engels foretold in *Pall Mall Gazette* that unless MacMahon succeeded in breaking through to Belgium with his army the iron ring of the German forces in the Sedan depression, which was closing ever tighter, would force him to capitulate. That is what actually did happen two weeks later.

After the defeat of the Paris Commune in 1871, the situation in the General Council of the International Working Men's Association became very difficult and strained, especially for Marx and Engels, who had still more work, as a large number of the International members of the Commune emigrated to London.

The Hungarian comrade Leo Frankel must not be forgotten: he had been a member of the Government of the Commune and had managed to get through the Prussian lines as a match seller. He was one of the few who were completely clear and conscious about their aim. Frankel returned to Paris after the amnesty and continued his propaganda there. He died a few years ago in Paris. In him I lost a personal friend and the Party, one of its best members. Respect to his memory!

The Commune emigrants, who belonged to different

trends, opposed one another and laid the blame for the downfall of the Commune on one another. The disappointed hopes and the difficult conditions in which nearly all of them were contributed more than anything else to the friction. The base attacks of the capitalist press and the general ignorance about the Commune and its significance and besides that the regrettable baiting from the anarchists—everything seemed to conspire to wipe out the international movement.

The transfer of the General Council to New York on the decision of the Hague Congress gave Marx and Engels time for their study of economics. Marx was able to devote himself entirely to his great work—*Capital*. From then on Engels was secretary of the International. Besides a number of articles on topics of actuality, translations of the *Communist Manifesto* or other translations which were sent for him to supervise or correct, not to speak of pamphlets for special occasions, took up a large part of his time. The number of scientific works our old friend nevertheless found time to write proves what a great capacity and love for work he had....

In 1878 a great sorrow struck Engels: his wife, an Irishwoman who had been heart and soul in the Sinn Fein movement, died. They had no children, and for Engels the loss of his wife was a heavy blow....

Then came sad times for the Marx family—Marx's illness, the illness of his wife and his daughter and the death of both of them.

In March 1883 came the not unexpected but all the same sorrowful news of Marx's death.

Engels wrote me the following letter:

"London, March 15, 1883

"Dear Lessner,

"Our old friend Marx closed his eyes for ever yesterday at three o'clock, softly and calmly. The immediate cause of his death was probably internal hemorrhage.

"The funeral will take place on Saturday at 12 o'clock. Tussy[1] requests your attendance.

"Excuse my haste.

"Yours, *F. Engels*."

---
[1] Eleanor Marx.—*Ed*.

Frederick Engels. 1864

May Day demonstration of the London workers in Hyde Park in 1892, at which Engels and Eleanor Marx were present

Barmen, birthplace of Frederick Engels

The place near Eastbourne where the ashes of Engels were consigned to the sea

After the death of Marx, Lenchen Demuth, who since Mrs. Marx's marriage had shared all the joys and sorrows of the Marx family for many years, ran Engels' household. She died on November 4, 1890. This was a great loss for Engels. Fortunately Mrs. Freyberger, formerly Mrs. Kautsky, decided shortly after to leave Vienna for London and take over Engels' household.

Who does not know that Engels eagerly took part in the new trade union movement and supported the eight-hour movement although he himself often worked sixteen hours a day and late into the night. He always attended the May celebrations in spite of his age and even climbed on to the cart that was used as a rostrum. And who can ever forget the May parties that followed those meetings?...

Engels' capacity and love for work persisted till his death. His great knowledge of foreign languages is well known. He knew ten languages thoroughly: he began to study Norwegian when he was over 70 years old in order to be able to read Ibsen and Kielland in the original.

Like Marx, Engels seldom made public speeches.... He spoke in public for the last time in 1893. He delivered addresses at the Zurich Congress, in Vienna and in Berlin. He was deeply moved, as he often told me later, by the reception and the spontaneous manifestations of gratitude and joy he was the object of in Zurich. His visit to Austria, Germany and Switzerland was a triumph for our ideas, and Engels often expressed regret that Marx had not lived to see the new Germany, the Germany of the workers.

Until his very death Engels showed as much calm as resolution and was simple and sincere in all his dealings. No matter what he was questioned about he always gave a brief but authoritative answer. He always spoke his mind frankly, whether people liked it or not.

When Engels disagreed with anything in the Party, he expressed his disapproval immediately and without reserve. He would have no part in shifts or compromises.... He received very many visits, Party comrades and others often coming to see him. When *Sozialdemokrat* had to move from Zurich to London at the end of the eighties the number of visits increased. Engels' house was still open to all.

After Marx's death I went to see Engels oftener. He showed me as much confidence as Marx had done. When he had too many visitors, I went to see him less often; he immediately asked me why he no longer saw so much of me.

4

Engels went to Eastbourne for his health for the last time in summer 1895. He came back without any improvement at the end of July. Tussy, who seemed very worried about him, informed me by letter. I made up my mind not to worry Engels with my visits for some time. I was afraid of exciting him by my presence, for he was very excitable by nature. As a result I never saw our great friend alive after his return to London.

On August 5, I was informed through Bernstein[1] that if I wanted to see Engels again before he died I must do so quickly, for his condition was very bad. I still had no idea that his death was so near, and I decided to go and see him the next day, August 6, as early as possible.

To my horror the first post next day brought me news from Mrs. Freyberger that our friend had died in the night of August 5 between 11 and 12.

I cannot convey in words the impression made upon me by that sad and unexpected news.... I immediately went to his house and found him lying dead on his bed, just as I had found our friend Marx on March 15, 1883.

Mrs. Freyberger, who took me into Engels' room, was so affected that she had difficulty in telling me about his last hours.

Engels' last will was that his ashes be sunk out at sea. This last desire was executed on August 27 by Eleanor Marx, Dr. E. Aveling, E. Bernstein and me. We went to Eastbourne, Engels' favourite summer resort, hired a two-oared boat and rowed about two miles out to sea with the urn containing the ashes of our unforgettable friend. I cannot express in words the feeling this trip produced in me....

---

[1] *Bernstein, Eduard* (1850-1932)—German Social-Democrat; after Engels' death renegade, advocated revision of Marxism.—*Ed.*

* * *

Marx and Engels have been departed for years; but their work lives. The millions of workers in all countries show that the principles as well as the tactics of our leaders in the fight are understood, grasped and followed, and the ranks of those workers are increasing every day....

This is an immense satisfaction for me, and I end these reminiscences by proclaiming with the millions of the proletarians:

"The immediate future belongs to the socialist movement!"

Friedrich Adolf Sorge

ON MARX[1]

On March 14, 1883, I got the following cable from London: "Marx died today. Engels."

The leader of the proletariat's struggle, the man who forged the weapons for the emancipation of the working class, was dead. The titanic mind which flashed lightning into the world, the bourgeois world, to dissipate the ignorance born of darkness and breeding darkness and to open up prospects of a new era and new conditions for the whole of mankind, had passed away.

Marx was dead, and millions mourned at the news that the heart of their most faithful and most reliable adviser had ceased to beat!

What Marx, the man of science and the defender of the working class, achieved does not need to be engraved on tables of bronze or celebrated in words of fire. No monument of metal or stone proclaims it, but the countless multitudes of the proletariat in all countries and all parts of the world feel it and know it, and prove it by the growth of their fighting ranks under the immortal slogan given them by Marx: "Proletarians of all countries, unite!"

Only a few people know what sacrifices Marx and the true companion of his life made to their convictions; how many privations and hardships they endured while he created his immortal works, blazed new paths in the most important branches of science and by his advice and his deeds helped all who genuinely and sincerely desired the advancement of the working class.

---

[1] *Sorge, Friedrich Adolf* (1828-1906)—German Communist who emigrated to America, participant in the American and international working-class movement; friend and associate of Marx and Engels.

These reminiscences were published in 1902.—*Ed.*

Despite this, calumny was ceaselessly spread against Marx, and aspersions were cast on the motives of his actions. That is why fifty years ago, on November 7, 1853, three of his old comrades-in-arms published a document,[1] a few passages of which are given here:

"Marx, as every one knows, has never bored the public with a single line about his own sacrifices for the revolution. On the contrary, nothing would have roused his indignation more than the pity of the petty bourgeois.... May the Party at least be informed of the worth of attacks on his person.

"Marx and Engels have worked gratis from 1843 to the present day for Owen's *New Moral World,* O'Connor's *Northern Star,* Harney's *Democratic Review, Republican* and *Friend of the People,* Jones' *Notes to the People* and *People's Paper,* the Paris *Réforme* (before the revolution), and a number of journals in Belgium and Paris (*Deutsche-Brüsseler Zeitung,* etc.).... In consideration of this, Flocon, a member of the Provisional Government, offered them both money at their discretion but they refused. Instead, Marx, as we well know, spent several thousand thalers of his own money at the outbreak of the February Revolution partly for the arming of the workers in Brussels, where a revolution was imminent, for which he and his wife were imprisoned by the Belgian authorities, partly to help friends to go to Germany and to prepare for the revolution there, and the rest for the initial costs of the *Neue Rheinische Zeitung.* In 1848 and 1849 Marx spent about 7,000 thalers on this newspaper and for revolutionary agitation, partly in cash from his own money and that of his wife, partly in deeds made out against his inheritance.

"How comes it that the newspaper used up a large part of these sacrifices? At the beginning, the number of shareholders was large, but when the June Revolution broke out and the *Neue Rheinische Zeitung* was at first the only newspaper in Germany to support it, the bourgeois naturally fell away from it. The desertion of the petty bourgeois took place after a state of siege was declared in Cologne. That is why Marx took over the newspaper from the sharehold-

---

[1] The letter written by Weydemeyer, Cluss and Jacoby to the *Belletristisches Journal und New-Yorker Criminal-Zeitung* was published on November 25, 1853.—*Ed.*

ers as his "personal property", that is, he took upon himself all its debts and liabilities.... When the paper was again paying it was suppressed by force. In May 1849, when Marx returned from a journey to Hamburg, his wife had already received his expulsion order....

"The paper was closed. Its assets consisted of 1) a steam printing press, 2) a newly set-up compositor's room, 3) 1,000 thalers subscription fees in the Post Office. Marx left all that in order to cover the paper's debts....

"With 300 thalers which he borrowed, Marx paid the type-setters and printers and enabled the editors to get away. Not a *pfennig* went into his own pocket....

"Thus Marx arrived in London in a sorry plight and it was only through his energy that he got out of it. If he was bankrupt when he arrived in London, it was the revolution that had made him bankrupt. If he did not amend his position earlier it was because he preferred to serve the workers gratis.... When one of his children died in London ... he had no money to pay for its burial....

"As a result, Marx, who with his family was used to better conditions and can and should live decently in the public eye, only managed with great difficulty and was moreover 'civilly' undermined by frauds:

"If the German Workers' Party allows men like Marx..., men who have sacrificed for it not only their work and their position, but their fortune and the comfort of their family, to be knavishly calumniated, then let each one pass sentence upon it.

"New York, November 7, 1853

"*J. Weydemeyer*,[1] *Adolf Cluss*,[2] *Dr. A. Jacoby*.[3]"

Marx has been accused of ambition and reproached with heartless, inhumane conduct. What injustice!

---

[1] *Weydemeyer, Joseph* (1818-1866)—prominent figure in the German and American working-class movement; took part in the 1848-49 revolution in Germany and the American Civil War; friend and associate of Marx and Engels.—*Ed.*

[2] *Cluss, Adolf*—German engineer, member of the Communist League; after 1849 emigrated to the U.S.A.—*Ed.*

[3] *Jacoby, Abraham* (1830-1919)—member of the Communist League, one of the accused at the Cologne Communist Trial; afterwards emigrated to the U.S.A.—*Ed.*

He never showed ambition or sought to dominate, and it was only thanks to his superior knowledge, his vast erudition, his all-round learning and his imposing character that he won the influence that he had, especially in the old General Council of the International in London, about four-fifths of which were Englishmen or Frenchmen, only two or three members being Germans in the most important period.

In Paris, Brussels, Cologne and London he spoke to workers and delivered addresses in workers' societies.... In the General Council too, he vindicated his views and proposals—which as a rule set the general line for the Council—with well-sustained arguments, the logic of which was irresistible even to his opponents. And not the logic alone, but the warmth of his tone too. The last sentences of *The Civil War in France* illustrate this.

In personal associations Marx was a friendly, pleasant, likable man, as all will agree who had the happiness of any close relations with this extraordinary man.

But he was relentless towards hypocrites, and ignorant or pretentious people, and it was these who blackened Marx's character and invented and spread the legend of his ambition, etc.

Anybody with Marx's experience of the hardships of life was always ready to help and did help when he could. Countless cases could be quoted. Let one suffice. When the Congress of the North-American Federation of the International Working Men's Association closed its session in July 1872 and elected delegates to the Hague Congress, a worker went up to one of those delegates and gave him a sum of money for Marx. He was a Rhineland worker, a strict follower of Lassalle, who had been obliged to leave his family and home in 1864 or 1865, had arrived in London penniless and asked Marx for help to continue his journey to America. Marx had helped him, although he was in by no means a good situation at the time.

When the emigrants of the Commune arrived in London Marx and his family made extraordinary efforts to help and support them. And besides the emigrants who came and went, one could often meet in his house workers from the provinces, from Manchester and Liverpool, from the continent, from America and other distant parts.

H. A. Lopatin

FROM A LETTER TO N. P. SINELNIKOV[1]

February 15, 1873

Most of my time abroad I spent in Paris or London, where I earned my living in the same capacity as in Russia—that of a literary day-worker. In my leisure hours I studied the working-class movement and other interesting aspects of social life abroad.

During my stay in London I came into contact with a certain Karl Marx, one of the most remarkable writers on political economy and one of the most widely educated men in the whole of Europe. Some five years ago it occurred to him to study Russian; having done so he came across Chernyshevsky's notes on Mill's famous treatise[2] and some other articles by Chernyshevsky. Marx read those articles and felt great respect for Chernyshevsky. He told me several times that Chernyshevsky was the only contemporary economist who had really original ideas, while all the others were in fact only compilers; that his works were full of originality, force and depth and were the only modern

---

[1] *Lopatin, Hermann Alexandrovich* (1845-1918)—Russian revolutionary, Narodnik, member of the General Council of the First International; friend of Marx and his family. Lopatin wrote this letter while in prison in Irkutsk. *Sinelnikov, Nikolai Petrovich* (1805-1894)—Governor-General of Eastern Siberia.—*Ed.*

[2] *Chernyshevsky, Nikolai Gavrilovich* (1828-1889)—great Russian revolutionary democrat, materialist philosopher, scientist, critic and writer.

Here the reference is to Chernyshevsky's book *Additions and Notes to John Stuart Mill's First Book on Political Economy*, Vol. III, Geneva 1869.—*Ed.*

works on that science which really deserved to be read and studied. He said the Russians should be ashamed that not one of them had so far cared to make such a wonderful thinker known in Europe and that the political death of Chernyshevsky was a loss for the world of science not only in Russia but in the whole of Europe, etc. Although I had so far greatly respected Chernyshevsky's works on political economy, my knowledge in that field was not broad enough to distinguish which thoughts were original and which ones he had taken from other authors. Naturally, such an opinion from a judge of Marx's competence only increased my respect for Chernyshevsky. And when I compared this opinion of him as a writer with the opinions on his great nobleness of character and personal self-sacrifice that I had heard from people who were closely acquainted with him and could never speak of him without profound emotion, I conceived a burning desire to give back to the world that great publicist and citizen, of whom, as Marx said, Russia should be proud. I could not bear to think that one of the best citizens of Russia, one of the most remarkable thinkers of his time, a man who deserved a place in the Russian Pantheon, was fated to a fruitless, miserable life of torment, buried away in some god-forsaken place in Siberia. I swear that I was ready then as I am now to change places with him without hesitation if I had been able and if by that sacrifice I could have returned to the cause of my country's progress one of its most influential protagonists. I would have done so without hesitating a second and with the same joyful readiness as a private soldier throws himself before his beloved general to protect him with his body. But that romantic dream was never to come true. At the same time, I then thought that there was another, more practical and feasible way of helping that man.[1] Judging by my own experience in similar circumstances and also by other cases I had heard of, I thought there was nothing essentially impossible in such an undertaking: all that was needed was a certain amount of fearless enterprise and a little money. So shortly afterwards I wrote and asked for the help of two of my personal friends in Petersburg and they offered to give me the necessary

---

[1] Lopatin intended to organise Chernyshevsky's escape from exile.—*Ed.*

money, accepting to be repaid in case of success but to forget all about it in case of failure. When I passed through Petersburg three of my friends there added somewhat to that sum, making a total of 1,085 rubles.

When I left London I did not even tell anybody where I was going, with the exception of the five men with whom I had corresponded earlier and from whom I had received money and also Elpidin in Geneva, who already knew of my intention before that through circumstances not worth mentioning. I did not even tell Marx of my venture, in spite of the closeness of my association with him and my friendship and respect for him. I was sure that he would consider me mad and would try to dissuade me, and I do not like to go back on an already well-considered step.

Not being acquainted with Chernyshevsky's relatives or his friends on the *Sovremennik* staff, I did not even know exactly where he was. Having no acquaintances in Siberia, or even any letters of introduction, I had to spend almost a month in Irkutsk before I found out what I needed. That long stay in Irkutsk, together with other blunders I committed and certain circumstances not depending upon me, attracted the attention of the local administration. What still more contributed to my failure, if I am not mistaken, was Elpidin's indiscretion, for he gave away the news of my departure for Siberia to a government detective living in Geneva. Whatever the case, I was arrested and found myself in prison for the fourth time. Seeing that my attempt had failed and that the prospects were not particularly pleasant for me and also noting that the court proceedings were being put off in the expectation that I would make certain confessions which I did not consider myself entitled to make, I attempted to escape but failed and was jailed in Irkutsk.[1]

---

[1] Lopatin escaped from Irkutsk prison for the first time on June 3, 1871, but was immediately recaptured. Only at the second attempt, on July 10, 1873, did he manage to make good his escape. In August 1873 he was already in Paris.—*Ed*.

Jenny Marx

SHORT SKETCH OF AN EVENTFUL LIFE[1]

June 19, 1843, was my wedding-day.
We went from Kreuznach to Rhein-Pfalz via Ebernburg and returned via Baden-Baden. Then we stayed at Kreuznach till the end of September. My dear mother returned to Trèves with my brother Edgar. Karl and I arrived in Paris in October and were met by Herwegh[2] and his wife.

In Paris Karl and Ruge edited the *Deutsch-Französische Jahrbücher,* Julius Fröbel being the publisher. The enterprise came to grief after the very first issue. We lived in rue Vanneau, Faubourg St. Germain.... There was a lot of gossip and quarrels over bagatelles. Our little Jenny was born on May 1, 1844. I went out for the first time after that to Laffitte's burial and six weeks later I took the mail coach to Trèves with my mortally sick child.... In September I returned to Paris with a German nurse. By then little Jenny had four teeth.

During my absence Karl had had a visit from Frederick Engels.... Suddenly, at the beginning of 1845, the police commissioner came to our house and showed us an expulsion order made out by Guizot on the request of the Prussian Government. "Karl Marx must leave Paris within

---

[1] Here we publish excerpts from the autobiographical notes by Marx's wife, Jenny, which date back to 1865. These notes were not intended for the press and therefore they are desultory in character but they are of great interest since they show Marx as a man and describe the hard conditions in which the Marx family lived.—*Ed.*

[2] *Herwegh, Georg* (1817-1875)—famous German poet, petty-bourgeois democrat.—*Ed.*

24 hours," the order ran. I was given a longer delay, which I made use of to sell my furniture and some of my linen. I got ridiculously little for it, but I had to find money for our journey. The Herweghs gave me hospitality for two days. Ill and in bitter cold weather, I followed Karl to Brussels at the beginning of February. There we put up at Bois Sauvage Hotel and I met Heinzen and Freiligrath for the first time. In May we moved into a small house that we rented from Dr. Breuer in rue de l'Alliance, outside Porte du Louvain.

Hardly had we settled down when we were followed by Engels.... Shortly afterwards Hess arrived with his wife, and a certain Sebastian Seiler joined the small German circle. He set up a correspondence bureau and the small German colony lived pleasantly together. Then we were joined by some Belgians, among them Gigot, and several Poles. In one of the attractive cafés that we went to in the evenings I made the acquaintance of old Lelewel[1] in his blue blouse.

During the summer Engels worked with Karl on the criticism of German philosophy.... The criticism was a bulky work and was to be published in Westphalia.

In the spring Joseph Weydemeyer paid us his first visit, remaining for some time as our guest. In April my dear Mother sent her own trusty maid to Brussels to help me. I went with her once more to see Mother, taking little Jenny who was then fourteen months old. I stayed with her six weeks and returned to our small colony two weeks before Laura was born, on September 26. My brother Edgar spent the winter with us in Brussels, hoping to find work there. He entered Seiler's correspondence bureau. Later, in spring 1846, our dear Wilhelm Wolff also joined the bureau. He was known as "Kasemattenwolff", having escaped from a fortress in Silesia where he had been four years for a violation of the law on the press. His coming to us was the beginning of the close friendship with our dear "Lupus"[2] that was dissolved only by his death in May 1864....

---

[1] *Lelewel, Joachim* (1786-1861)—outstanding Polish revolutionary, participant in the Polish insurrection of 1830-31; subsequently emigrated from Poland.—*Ed.*

[2] *Lupus*—Wilhelm Wolff. *Lupus* in Latin means "wolf", the German "Wolff" also meaning "wolf".—*Ed.*

In the meantime the storm-clouds of the revolution had been piling higher and higher. The Belgian horizon too was dark. What was feared above all was the workers, the social element of the popular masses. The police, the military, the civil guard, all were called out against them, all were kept ready for action. Then the German workers decided that it was time to arm themselves too. Daggers, revolvers, etc., were procured. Karl willingly provided money, for he had just come into an inheritance. In all this the government saw conspiracy and criminal plans: Marx receives money and buys weapons, he must therefore be got rid of. Late at night two men broke into our house. They asked for Karl: when he appeared they said they were police sergeants and had a warrant to arrest him and take him to be questioned. They took him away. I hurried after him in terrible anxiety and went to influential men to find out what the matter was. I rushed from house to house in the dark. Suddenly I was seized by a guard, arrested and thrown into a dark prison. It was where beggars without a home, vagabonds and wretched fallen women were detained. I was thrust into a dark cell. As I entered, sobbing, an unhappy companion in misery offered to share her place with me: it was a hard plank bed. I lay down on it. When morning broke I saw at the window opposite mine, behind iron bars, a cadaverous, mournful face. I went to the window and recognised our good old friend Gigot. When he saw me he beckoned to me, pointing downwards. I looked in that direction and saw Karl being led away under military escort. An hour later I was taken to the interrogating magistrate. After a two hours' questioning, during which they got little out of me, I was led to a carriage by gendarmes and towards evening I got back to my three poor little children. The affair caused a great sensation. All the papers reported on it. After a short while Karl too was released and ordered to leave Brussels immediately.

He had already intended to return to Paris and had applied to the Provisional Government in France for a repeal of the expulsion order issued against him under Louis Philippe. He at once received a paper signed by Flocon by which the Provisional Government cancelled the expulsion order in very flattering terms. So Paris was open to us again. Where could we feel more at ease than under the rising sun of the new revolution? We had to go there, we just had to! I hastily packed my belongings and sold what I could, but left my boxes with all my silver-plate and my best linen in Brussels in charge of the bookseller Vögler, who was particularly helpful and obliging during the preparations for my departure.

Thus we left Brussels after being there for three years. It was a cold, dull day and we had difficulty in keeping the children warm, the youngest of them was just a year old....

* * *

At the end of May[1] Karl put out the last issue of the *Neue Rheinische Zeitung,* printed in red—the famous "red number", a real fire-brand in form and content. Engels had immediately joined the Baden rising in which he was adjutant to Willich. Karl made up his mind to go to Paris again for a while, as it was impossible for him to stay on in Germany.[2] Red Wolff followed him there. I went with the three children via Bingen ... to see my old home town and my dear Mother. I made a detour a little after Bingen in order to convert into ready money the silver-plate which I had just redeemed from the pawnbroker's in Brussels. Weydemeyer and his wife again gave us hospitality and were very helpful to me in my dealings with the pawnbroker. Thus I managed again to get money for the journey.

Karl went with Red Wolff to Baden-Pfalz and then on to Paris.... Reaction came on the scene in all its fury everywhere. The Hungarian revolution, the Baden insurrection, the Italian rising, all collapsed. Courts-martial were rife in Hungary and Baden. During the presidency of Louis Napoleon, who was elected with an enormous majority at the end of 1848, 50,000 Frenchmen entered the "city of the seven hills" and occupied Italy.[3] *"L'ordre règne à Varsovie"* and *"Vae victis!"* were the mottos of the counter-revolution

---

[1] 1849.—*Ed.*

[2] Profiting by the fact that Marx had relinquished Prussian citizenship in 1845, the government expelled him in May 1849 as a "foreigner" who had violated the "law of hospitality".—*Ed.*

[3] Allusion to the French armed intervention against the Roman Republic in 1849. Its aim was to restore the temporal power of the Pope.—*Ed.*

in the elation of victory. The bourgeoisie breathed relieved, the petty bourgeois went back to their business, the liberal petty philistines clenched their fists in their pockets, the workers were hounded and persecuted and the men who fought with sword and pen for the reign of the poor and oppressed were glad to be able to earn their bread abroad.

While in Paris Karl established contacts with many of the leaders of clubs and secret workers' societies. I followed him to Paris in July 1849 and we stayed there a month. But we were to get no rest there either. One fine day the familiar police sergeant came again and informed us that "Karl Marx and his wife had to leave Paris within 24 hours". By an act of clemency he was given permission to take up his residence in Vannes, in the Morbihan.

Karl did not, of course, accept such an exile. I packed my goods and chattels again to look for a sure place of rest in London. Karl hastened there ahead of me and established close contact with Blind.[1] Georg Weerth[2] also came later on. It was he who met me when I arrived, sick and exhausted with my three poor persecuted small children. He found accommodation for me in a boarding-house in Leicester Square belonging to a master-tailor. We looked in haste for a larger lodging in Chelsea, for the time was approaching when I would need a quiet roof over my head. On November 5,[3] while the people outside were shouting "Guy Fawkes for ever!", small masked boys were riding the streets on cleverly made donkeys and all was in an uproar, my poor little Heinrich was born. We called him Little Fawkes, in honour of the great conspirator.

Shortly afterwards Engels also arrived in London via Genoa, fleeing from Baden....

Thousands of emigrants arrived daily. Few of them had any means of their own, all were in more or less dire straits, needing and looking for help. This was one of the most unpleasant periods of our life in emigration. Emigrant com-

---

[1] *Blind, Karl* (1826-1907)—German publicist, took part in the Baden revolutionary movement in 1848-49; in the 1850s was one of the leaders of the German emigrants in London.—*Ed.*

[2] *Weerth, Georg* (1822-1856)—German proletarian poet and publicist, member of the Communist League; friend of Marx and Engels.—*Ed.*

[3] *November 5*—the day of the "gunpowder plot" celebrated annually in England (see footnote on p. 86 of this book).—*Ed.*

mittees were founded to help them, meetings were arranged, appeals made, programmes drawn up and great demonstrations prepared. In all emigrant circles dissensions broke out. The various parties gradually split up completely. It came to an official separation between the German Democrats on the one hand and the socialists on the other, and there was a clear rift even among the communist working men....

Karl had started negotiations in the autumn of 1849 for a new journal to be edited in London and published in Hamburg. The first 3 or 4 issues appeared after countless difficulties under the title: *Revue der Neuen Rheinischen Zeitung*. It was a great success, but the bookseller, bought over by the German Government, was so negligent and inefficient over the business side of it that it was soon obvious that it could not go on for long.

In the spring of 1850 we were forced to leave our Chelsea house. My poor little Fawkes was always ill and the anxieties about our daily life were also ruining my health. Harassed on all sides and pursued by creditors, we put up for a week in a German hotel in Leicester Square. But we did not stay there long. One morning our worthy host refused to serve us our breakfast and we were forced to look for other lodgings. The small help I got from my Mother often saved us from the bitterest privations. We found two rooms in the house of a Jewish lace dealer and spent a miserable summer there with the four children.

That autumn Karl and some of his closest friends broke completely off from the doings of the bulk of the emigrants and never took part in a single demonstration. He and his friends left the Workers' Educational Society.... Engels, after trying in vain to earn his living by writing in London, went to Manchester and worked as a clerk in his father's textile business on very hard terms. All our other friends tried to pay their way by giving lessons, etc. This and the next two years were for us a time of the greatest hardships, of continual acute anxiety, great privations of all kinds and actual need.

In August 1850, although I was not at all well, I made up my mind to leave my sick child and go to Holland to get consolation and help from Karl's uncle. I was desperate at the prospect of a fifth child and of the future. Karl's uncle was very ill-disposed by the unfavourable effect the revolution had had on his business and his sons'. He was embittered against the revolution and revolutionaries and in a very bad temper. He refused to give me any help. However, as I was going he pressed into my hand a present for my youngest child and I saw that it hurt him not to be able to give me more. The old man could not realise my feelings as I took leave of him. I returned home in despair. My poor little Edgar came leaping towards me with his friendly face and Little Fawkes stretched his tiny arms out to me. I was not to enjoy his caresses for long. In November the child died from convulsions caused by pneumonia. My sorrow was great. He was the first child I had lost. I had no idea then what other sufferings were in store for me which would make all others seem as nothing. Shortly after the child had been laid to rest we left the small flat for another one in the same street....

On March 28, 1851, our daughter Franzisca was born. We gave the poor little thing to a nurse, for we could not rear her with the others in three small rooms.... 1851 and 1852 were the years of the greatest and at the same time the most paltry troubles, worries, disappointments and privations of all kinds.

In the early summer 1851 an event occurred which I do not wish to relate here in detail, although it greatly contributed to increase our worries, both personal and others. During the spring the Prussian Government charged all Karl's friends in the Rhine province with the most dangerous revolutionary intrigues. They were all thrown into prison and treated in the most appalling way. The public trial did not start until the end of 1852. That was the famous Cologne Communist Trial. All the accused except Daniels and Jacoby were sentenced to from 3 to 5 years prison....

* * *

At first W. Pieper was Karl's secretary, but soon I took over that post. The memory of the days I spent in his little study copying his scrawly articles is among the happiest of my life.

Louis Napoleon's *coup d'état* took place at the end of 1851 and the following year Karl wrote his *Eighteenth Brumaire,* which was published in New York. He wrote the book in our small lodgings in Dean Street amidst the noise of the children and the household bustle. By March I had copied the manuscript out and it was sent off, but it did not appear in print till much later and brought in next to nothing.

At Easter, 1852, our little Franzisca had a severe bronchitis. For three days she was between life and death. She suffered terribly. When she died we left her lifeless little body in the back room, went into the front room and made our beds on the floor. Our three living children lay down by us and we all wept for the little angel whose livid, lifeless body was in the next room. Our beloved child's death occurred at the time of the hardest privations, our German friends being unable to help us just then. Ernest Jones, who paid us long and frequent visits about that time, promised to help us but he was unable to bring us anything.... Anguish in my heart, I hurried to a French emigrant who lived not far away and used to come to see us, and begged him to help us in our terrible necessity. He immediately gave me two pounds with the most friendly sympathy. That money was used to pay for the coffin in which my child now rests in peace. She had no cradle when she came into the world and for a long time was refused a last resting place. With what heavy hearts we saw her carried to her grave!

In August 1852 the trial of the Communists, since become famous, came to an end. Karl wrote a pamphlet disclosing the infamy of the Prussian Government. It was printed in Switzerland by Schabelitz but was confiscated at the frontier by the Prussian Government and destroyed. Cluss had it printed again in America and many copies of the new edition were spread on the continent.

During the year 1853 Karl used to write two articles regularly for the *New York Daily Tribune*. They attracted great attention in America. This steady income enabled us to pay off our old debts to a certain extent and to live a less anxious life. The children grew up nicely, developing both physically and mentally, although we were still living in the poky Dean Street flat....

Christmas that year was the first merry feast we celebrated in London. We were relieved from nagging daily worries by Karl's connection with the *New York Tribune*. The children had romped about more in the open air in the parks during the summer. There had been cherries, strawberries and even grapes that year, and our friends brought our three little ones all sorts of delightful presents: dolls, guns, cooking utensils, drums and trumpets. Dronke[1] came late in the evening to decorate the Christmas tree. It was a happy evening.

A week later our little Edgar showed the first symptoms of the incurable disease which was to lead to his death a year later. Had we been able to give up our small unhealthy flat then and take the child to the seaside, we might have saved him. But what is done cannot be undone....

In September 1855 we returned to our old headquarters in Dean Street, firmly resolved to move out as soon as a small English inheritance freed us from the chains and ties in which the baker, butcher, milkman, grocer and greengrocer and all the other "hostile forces" held us. At last, in spring 1856 we received the small sum that was to release us. We paid all our debts, redeemed our silver, linen and clothes from the pawnbroker's and I went newly clothed with my little ones to my beloved old home for the last time....

We spent that winter in great retirement. Nearly all our friends had left London and the few that remained lived a long way from us. Besides, our attractive little house, though it was like a palace for us in comparison with the places we had lived in before, was not easy to get to. There was no smooth road leading to it, building was going all around, one had to pick one's way over heaps of rubbish and in rainy weather the sticky red soil caked to one's boots so that it was after a tiring struggle and with heavy feet that one reached our house. And then it was dark in those wild districts, so that rather than have to tackle the dark, the rubbish, the clay and the heaps of stones one preferred to spend the evenings by a warm fire.

I was very unwell that winter and was always surrounded with stacks of medicine bottles and it was a long time before I could get used to the complete solitude. I often missed the long walks I had been in the habit of making in the crowded West-End streets, the meetings, the clubs and our favourite public-house and homely conversations which had so often helped me to forget the worries of life for a time. Luckily I still had the article for the *Tribune* to copy out twice a week and that kept me in touch with world events.

---

[1] *Dronke, Ernest* (1822-1891)—German publicist, one of the editors of the *Neue Rheinische Zeitung*; after the 1848-49 revolution withdrew from political activity.—*Ed.*

In the middle of 1857 another great trade crisis faced the American workers. The *Tribune* again declined to pay for two articles a week and as a result there was another considerable ebb in our budget. Luckily Dana was then publishing an encyclopaedia and Karl was asked to write articles on military and economic questions. But as such articles were very irregular and the growing children and the larger house led to greater expenses, this was by no means a time of prosperity. It was not positive need, but we were permanently hard up and worried by petty fears and calculations. No matter how much we cut down expenses, we could never make ends meet and our debts mounted from day to day and year to year. . . .

On July 6 the seventh child was born to us, but it lived only long enough to breathe a while and then be carried to join its brothers and sisters. . . .

In spring 1860 Engels' father died. After that Engels' situation considerably improved although he remained bound by the unfavourable contract signed with Ermen, which was valid until 1864, from which time Engels became a co-partner in the management of the firm.

In August 1860, I again spent a fortnight at Hastings with the children. On my return I began to copy the book Karl had written against Vogt and his associates. It was printed in London and did not appear till the end of December 1860 after much annoyance. At the time I was very ill with pox, having just recovered enough from the terrible disease to be able to devour *Herr Vogt* with half blinded eyes. That was a most dismal time. The three children had found a home and hospitality with the faithful Liebknecht.

Just then appeared the first forebodings of the great American Civil War that was to break out the next spring. Old Europe with its petty, old-fashioned pigmy-struggles ceased to interest America. The *Tribune* informed Karl that it was forced by financial circumstances to forgo all correspondence and that it would not need his collaboration for the time being. The blow was felt all the more as all other sources of income had completely dried up and all efforts to undertake something had proved to be failures. The hardest thing about it was that this complete helplessness came as our eldest daughters entered the beautiful golden age of maidenhood. So we had again to fight the same sorrows, troubles and privations as of old, the difference being that what the children had been unconscious of at the age of five and six, they had consciously to bear up with ten years later when they were fifteen and sixteen. Thus we learned in practice the German proverb "Small children, small troubles, big children, big troubles".

In the summer of 1860 we took in Eccarius for two months, for he was very poorly. In spring 1861 Karl went to Germany because it was absolutely necessary to get financial help. The King of Prussia, called the "genial", had died at Christmas and left his throne to "handsome Wilhelm".[1] The corporal proclaimed an amnesty and Karl availed himself of it to make a trip to Germany and see the new lie of the land. In Berlin he lived at Lassalle's and saw a lot of Countess Hatzfeldt.[2] Then he went to Holland to visit his uncle Leon Philips who had the real magnanimity to advance him a sum of money interest-free. Karl came home accompanied by Jacques Philips von Bommel just in time for Jennychen's seventeenth birthday. The loan put our finances afloat and we sailed on for a time happily, although always between rocks and sand-banks, drifting between Charybdis and Scylla.

Our eldest daughters left school in the summer of 1860 and attended only a few lessons held in the college for non-pupils too. They continued to learn French and Italian with M. de Colme and Signor Maggioni and Jenny also took drawing lessons with Mr. Oldfield until 1862. In autumn the girls began to take singing lessons with Mr. Henry Banner....

Jenny's health was poor during the whole of spring 1863 and she was continually under the care of doctors. Karl was also extremely unwell. He was no better when he came back from a visit to Engels, one of his regular annual visits since 1850. We again spent three weeks at the seaside at Hastings, being with H. Banner twelve days. Karl came to fetch us but he looked very bad and continually felt unwell, until in November of that year it turned out that he had terrible illness called the "carbuncle disease". On November 10 a terrible abscess was opened and he was in danger for a fairly long time afterwards. The disease lasted a good four weeks and

---

[1] In 1861 Frederick-William IV of Prussia died and was succeeded by William I.—*Ed.*

[2] *Hatzfeldt, Sophie* (1805-1881)—friend and follower of Ferdinand Lassalle.—*Ed.*

caused severe physical sufferings. These were accompanied by rankling moral tortures of all kinds.... The doctor decided that a change of air would be very beneficial for Karl, and on his advice Karl, although not yet quite recovered, left in the middle of the winter cold for Germany accompanied by our anxious and heartfelt wishes in order to see to his mother's legacy in Trèves. He stayed there a short time with his brother-in-law Conradi and sister Emilie and then made a detour to Frankfurt to see his aunt, his father's sister. From there he went to Bommel to see his uncle. He was very well looked after by his uncle and Nettchen. For unfortunately he required medical attention and careful nursing again, the illness, which had not been cured, breaking out very badly again as soon as he reached Bommel and forcing him to remain in Holland from Christmas until February 19.

That lonely disconsolate winter was terrible! The small share in the legacy that Karl brought back in ready money enabled us to free ourselves from obligations, debts, pawnbroker, etc. We were lucky enough to find a very attractive and healthy dwelling which we fitted out very comfortably and relatively smartly. At Easter 1864 we moved into the pleasant sunny house with the spacious airy rooms.

On May 2, 1864, we received a letter from Engels telling us that our good and faithful old friend Lupus was seriously ill. Karl hastened to go and see him and his faithful friend recognised him for a while. On May 9 Lupus breathed his last. In his will he made Karl, the children and myself his main legatees along with a few minor ones. It turned out that by his excessive industry and effort the homely, simply living man had saved up the appreciable sum of £1,000. He did not have the consolation of enjoying the fruit of his life in a quiet, comfortable old age. He afforded us help and relief and a year free from worry. A stay at the seaside was absolutely necessary for Karl's health, which was still precarious. He went to Ramsgate with Jenny, Laura and Tussy followed later....

During the year he managed to find a publisher for his big work on economics.[1] Meissner in Hamburg promised to publish it on fairly favourable conditions. Karl is now working intensely to finish the book....

---

[1] *Capital.—Ed.*

JENNY MARX TO JOSEPH WEYDEMEYER

London, May 20, 1850

Dear Herr Weydemeyer,

It will soon be a year since I was given such friendly and cordial hospitality by you and your dear wife, since I felt so comfortably at home in your house. All that time I have not given you a sign of life: I was silent when your wife wrote me such a friendly letter and did not even break that silence when we received the news of the birth of your child. My silence has often oppressed me, but most of the time I was unable to write and even today I find it hard, very hard.

Circumstances, however, force me to take up my pen. I beg you *to send us as soon as possible any money that has been or will be received* from the *Revue*.[1] *We need it very, very much.* Certainly nobody can reproach us with ever having made much case of the sacrifices we have been making and bearing for years, the public has never or almost never been informed of our circumstances; my husband is very sensitive in such matters and he would rather sacrifice his last than resort to democratic begging like officially recognised "great men". But he could have expected active and energetic support for his *Revue* from his friends, particularly those in Cologne. He could have expected such support first of all from where his sacrifices for the *Rheinische Zeitung* were known. But instead of that the business has been completely ruined by negligent and disorderly management, and one cannot say whether the delays of the bookseller or of the business managers or acquaintances in Cologne or the attitude of the democrats on the whole were the most ruinous.

---

[1] *Neue Rheinische Zeitung. Politisch-ökonomische Revue.—Ed.*

Here my husband is almost overwhelmed with the paltry worries of life in so revolting a form that it has taken all his energy, all his calm, clear, quiet sense of dignity to maintain him in that daily, hourly struggle. You know, dear Herr Weydemeyer, the sacrifices my husband has made for the paper. He put thousands in cash into it, he took over proprietorship, talked into it by worthy democrats who would otherwise have had to answer for the debts themselves, at a time when there was little prospect of success. To save the paper's political honour and the civic honour of his Cologne acquaintances he took upon himself the whole responsibility; he sacrificed his printing-press, he sacrificed all income, and before he left he even borrowed 300 thalers to pay the rent of the newly hired premises and the outstanding salaries of the editors, etc. And he was to be turned out by force. You know that we kept nothing for ourselves. I went to Frankfurt to pawn my silver—the last that we had—and I had my furniture in Cologne sold because I was in peril of having my linen and everything sequestrated. At the beginning of the unhappy period of the counter-revolution my husband went to Paris and I followed him with my three children. Hardly had he settled down in Paris when he was expelled and even my children and I were refused permission to reside there any longer. I followed him again across the sea. A month later our fourth child was born. You have to know London and conditions here to understand what it means to have three children and give birth to a fourth. For rent alone we had to pay 42 thalers a month. We were able to cope with this out of money which we received, but our meagre resources were exhausted when the *Revue* was published. Contrary to the agreement, we were not paid, and later only in small sums, so that our situation here was most alarming.

I shall describe to you just *one* day of that life, exactly as it was, and you will see that few emigrants, perhaps, have gone through anything like it. As wet-nurses here are too expensive I decided to feed my child myself in spite of continual terrible pains in the breast and back. But the poor little angel drank in so much worry and hushed-up anxiety that he was always poorly and suffered horribly day and night. Since he came into the world he has not slept a single night, two or three hours at the most and that rarely. Recently he has had violent convulsions, too, and has always been between

Karl Marx. 1875

Workers' strike at the Creusot metal plant in 1870

life and death. In his pain he sucked so hard that my breast was chafed and the skin cracked and the blood often poured into his trembling little mouth. I was sitting with him like that one day when our housekeeper came in. We had paid her 250 thalers during the winter and had an agreement to give the money in the future not to her but to her landlord, who had a bailiff's warrant against her. She denied the agreement and demanded five pounds that we still owed her. As we did not have the money at the time (Naut's letter did not arrive until later) two bailiffs came and sequestrated all my few possessions—linen, beds, clothes—everything, even my poor child's cradle and the best toys of my daughters, who stood there weeping bitterly. They threatened to take everything away in two hours. I would then have had to lie on the bare floor with my freezing children and my bad breast. Our friend Schramm hurried to town to get help for us. He got into a cab, but the horses bolted and he jumped out and was brought bleeding back to the house, where I was wailing with my poor shivering children.

We had to leave the house the next day. It was cold, rainy and dull. My husband looked for accommodation for us. When he mentioned the four children nobody would take us in. Finally a friend helped us, we paid our rent and I hastily sold all my beds to pay the chemist, the baker, the butcher and the milkman who, alarmed at the sight of the sequestration, suddenly besieged me with their bills. The beds which we had sold were taken out and put on a cart. What was happening? It was well after sunset. We were contravening English law. The landlord rushed up to us with two constables, maintaining that there might be some of his belongings among the things, and that we wanted to make away abroad. In less than five minutes there were two or three hundred persons loitering around our door—the whole Chelsea mob. The beds were brought in again—they could not be delivered to the buyer until after sunrise next day. When we had sold all our possessions we were in a position to pay what we owed to the last farthing. I went with my little darlings to the two small rooms we are now occupying in the German Hotel, 1, Leicester St., Leicester Square. There for £5 a week we were given a human reception.

Forgive me, dear friend, for being so long and wordy in describing a single day of our life here. It is indiscreet, I know, but my heart is bursting this evening, and I must at least once unload it to my oldest, best and truest friend. Do not think that these paltry worries have bowed me down: I know only too well that our struggle is not an isolated one and that I, in particular, am one of the chosen, happy, favoured ones, for my dear husband, the prop of my life, is still at my side. What really tortures my very soul and makes my heart bleed is that he had to suffer so much from paltry things, that so little could be done to help him, and that he who willingly and gladly helped so many others was so helpless himself. But do not think, dear Herr Weydemeyer, that we make demands on anybody. The only thing that my husband could have asked of those to whom he gave his ideas, his encouragement and his support was to show more energy in business and more support for his *Revue*. I am proud and bold to make that assertion. That little was his due. I do not think that would have been unfair to anybody. That is what grieves me. But my husband is of a different opinion. Never, not even in the most frightful moments, did he lose his confidence in the future or even his cheery humour, and he was satisfied when he saw me cheerful and our loving children cuddling close to their dear mother. He does not know, dear Herr Weydemeyer, that I have written to you in such detail about our situation. That is why I ask you not to refer to these lines. All he knows is that I have asked you in his name to hasten as much as you can the collection and sending of our money.

Farewell, dear friend. Give your wife my most affectionate remembrances and kiss your little angel for a mother who has shed many a tear over her baby. Our three eldest children are doing splendidly for all that, for all that. The girls are pretty, healthy, cheerful and good, and our chubby little boy is full of good humour and the most amusing notions. The little goblin sings the whole day long with astonishing feeling in a thunderous voice. The house shakes when he rings out in a fearful voice the words of Freiligrath's Marseillaise:

> Come, June, and bring us noble feats!
> To deeds of fame our heart aspires.

...Farewell!

JENNY MARX TO LUISE WEYDEMEYER

Hampstead, March 11, 1861

Dear Mrs. Weydemeyer,

I received your kind letter this morning and to show you how glad I was I wish to sit down and write you a long letter at once, for I know from your friendly letter that you like to hear from us sometimes and still have friendly memories of us, as we have of you. And how could such old Party comrades and friends that destiny has brought about the same sorrows and joys, the same sunny and gloomy days, ever feel estranged though time and the ocean separate them. So I stretch out my hand to you from afar as to a brave and faithful companion in sorrow, a fighter and a sufferer. Yes, dear Mrs. Weydemeyer, our hearts have often been heavy and sad, and I can well imagine what you must have gone through recently. I can imagine all your struggles, worries and privations, for I have often suffered the same myself. But suffering steels us and love keeps us up!

We had a bitterly hard time in the first years of our stay here, but I do not wish to dwell today on all the melancholy memories and all the losses we have suffered, nor on the sweet departed loves whose images we still carry in silent grief in our hearts.

Let me tell you today about a new period in our lives, which has had more than one sunny spell as well as cloudy days.

In 1856 I went to Trier with the three girls. My dear mother's joy was too great for words when I arrived with her grandchildren. But unfortunately it did not last long. That truest and best of mothers fell ill and after eleven days' suffering bestowed her blessing on the children and me and closed her dear tired eyes. Your dear husband, who knew how affectionate my mother was, will best be able to fathom my bereavement. When we had laid her beloved head in its last resting-place I saw to my mother's modest legacy, dividing it between my brother Edgar and myself, and then we left Trier. So far we had lived in London, in miserable furnished rooms. With the few hundred thalers that Mother had left us after all her sacrifices for us, we rented a small house not far from beautiful Hampstead Heath and we still live there now. It is a truly princely dwelling compared with the holes we used to live in, and although it did not cost us more than £40 to furnish it from top to bottom (second-hand junk helped a lot) I really felt magnificent at first in our snug parlour. All the linen and other small remains of past grandeur were redeemed from "Uncle's" and I again had the pleasure of counting the old Scottish damask napkins. Although the wonder did not last long—for one article after another soon had to go back to the pop-house—it was a real pleasure for us to be comfortable. Then came the first American crisis and our income was halved. We were again hard up and fell into debt. This could not be avoided because we had to carry on the education of the three girls as it had been begun.

Now I come to the bright aspect of our existence, the light side of our life—our dear children. I am sure that if your kind husband loved our daughters when they were children it would be a real joy for him to see them now that they have grown into budding maidens. I must now run the risk of your taking me for a doting mother by singing the praises of my darling daughters. They both have a very kind heart and good nature, really lovable modesty and maidenly virtue. Jenny will be seventeen on May 1. She is particularly attractive, and even pretty, with thick, dark, glossy hair, equally dark, shining, gentle eyes and a dark, creole complexion which, however, has a typically English freshness. The pleasant, good-natured expression of her apple-round childish face makes one overlook the not so pretty turned-up nose and it is a pleasure when the smiling mouth opens and shows her beautiful teeth.

Laura, who was fifteen years old last September, is perhaps prettier and has more regular features than her sister and is a direct contrast to her. She is just as tall, as slim and as delicately built as Jenny, but she is in all respects fairer, lighter and more limpid. You could call the upper part of her face beautiful, so charming is her wavy chestnut hair, so sweet her lovely green-shimmering eyes, always sparkling with joy, so noble and well-shaped her brow. But the lower part of her face is not so regular and has not yet reached full development. Both sisters have a truly blooming complexion and they are so free from any vanity that I often admire them in silence, all the more as the same could not be said of their mother when she was younger and still in flowing frocks.

At school they always won the first prizes. They are quite at home in English and know a fair amount of French. They understand Dante in Italian and can read a little in Spanish. It is only with German that they have big difficulties, although I do all I can to give them a lesson now and then; but they are not at all keen and I have no great authority with them or they much respect for me. Jenny is particularly good at drawing and her pencil drawings are the best ornaments in our rooms. Laura was so negligent as regards drawing that we discontinued her lessons to punish her. On the other hand, she applies herself to piano exercises and sings duets with her sister very charmingly in English and in German. Unfortunately it was not until late—about a year and a half ago—that they were able to begin taking music lessons. It was beyond our means to play for them and, besides, we had no piano. The one we have now is only hired and is hardly worth calling a piano. Both the girls give us many a joy because of their lovable, modest disposition. But their younger sister is petted and pampered by the whole house.

The child was born just as my poor dear Edgar was taken away from us and all the love for the little brother, all affection for him, was transferred to the baby sister. The elder girls fostered and fondled her with almost motherly care. It is true that there can hardly be a more lovable child, so pretty, simple and good-humoured. The most striking thing about her is her love for talking and telling stories. This she got from the Grimm Brothers, with whom she does not part night or day. We all read her those tales till we are weary, but woe betide us if we leave out a single syllable about the Noisy Goblin, King Brosselbart or Snow-White. It is through these tales that the child has learned German, besides English which she breathes here with the air, and that her speech is most correct and precise. She is Karl's real pet and her chatter dispels many of his worries.

As far as the household is concerned, Lenchen is still as steadfast and conscientious as ever. Ask your husband about her, he will tell you what a treasure she has been for me. She has sailed with us through fair and foul for sixteen years. . . .

Hardly had I finished copying the manuscript—it was still at the press—when I suddenly began to feel very poorly. A terrible fever came over me and a doctor had to be called in. He came on November 20 and examined me at length and with great care. After a long silence he said to me: "My dear Mrs. Marx, I am sorry to say you have got the smallpox —the children must leave the house immediately." You can imagine the terror and the wailing that these words caused in the house. What could we do? The Liebknechts did not hesitate to take in our children and that very noon the girls, carrying their few belongings, went into exile.

I got worse from hour to hour, pockmarks broke out fearfully. I was in great suffering. I had severe burning pains in my face and was completely unable to sleep. I was mortally anxious about Karl, who took the most tender care of me. In the end I lost all use of my outward senses although I was fully conscious all the time. I lay constantly by the open window so that the cold November air would blow over me, while there was a raging fire in the stove and ice on my burning lips, and I was given drops of claret from time to time. I could hardly swallow, my hearing was getting weaker, and finally my eyes closed, so that I did not know whether I would remain enveloped in eternal night.

My constitution, helped by the tenderest and truest care, took the upper hand, however, and so I am sitting here now in perfect health but with my face disfigured by pockmarks and of a red which is just the "Magenta" that is now in fashion. The children were not allowed back to the paternal home that they had been so longing for until Christmas eve. Our reunion was indescribably moving. The girls were overwhelmed with emotion and could hardly keep back their tears when they saw me. Five weeks before I had looked quite respectable beside my healthy-looking girls. Surprisingly, I had no grey hair and my teeth and figure were good and therefore people used to class me among the well-preserved women. But that was all a thing of the past now and I seemed to myself a kind of cross between a rhinoceros and a hippopotamus whose place was in the zoo rather than among the members of the Caucasian race. But do not be too terrified. It is not so bad now, the marks are beginning to heal.

No sooner was I able to leave my bed than my dear Karl fell ill. The excessive anxiety, worries and torments of all sorts forced him to take to his bed. His chronic liver disease took an acute turn for the first time. But thank God he got better after four weeks' suffering. In the meantime the *Tribune* had again halved our income and instead of getting money for Karl's book we had to pay a bill of exchange. Added to that came all the enormous expenses of that terrible disease. In a word, you can imagine our situation that winter.

As a result of all this Karl decided to make a flying trip to Holland, the land of his fathers, tobacco and cheese. He wants to see whether he can get any money out of his uncle. So I am a grass widow for the time being, waiting for what success the trip to Holland will bring. On Saturday I got the first letter with some hope and sixty gulden. Such a matter cannot, of course, be hurried; tact, diplomacy and skill must be used. All the same, I hope that Karl will manage to rake something together there. As soon as he has any success in Holland he wants to make a secret detour to Berlin to see the lie of the land and if possible to arrange a monthly or weekly journal. We have been only too well convinced by late experiences that no progress is possible unless we have our own paper. If Karl succeeds in founding a new Party paper he will certainly write to your husband to ask him for reports from America.

Almost immediately after Karl's departure our faithful Lenchen fell ill and she is still in bed, though on the way to recovery. So I have my hands full and have written off this letter in the greatest hurry. But I was unable and unwilling to remain silent, and it has done my heart good to have emptied it to my oldest and truest friends. That is why I do not beg your pardon for having written at such great length about everything. My pen ran away with me and I only hope and wish that these scribbled lines will bring you some of the pleasure I had in reading your letter.

I immediately settled the matter of the bill of exchange and put everything in order just as if my lord and master had been here.

My daughters send love and kisses to your children—one Laura to the other—and I send each of them a kiss. Friendliest remembrances to your dear self. Be brave and courageous in these hard times. The world belongs to the fearless. Be a faithful and firm support for your husband and keep agile in body and in mind and the true "unrespectful" comrade of your dear children. And let us hear from you again when the occasion offers.

Yours,
Jenny Marx

Eleanor Marx-Aveling

KARL MARX[1]

(A Few Stray Notes)

My Austrian friends ask me to send them some recollections of my father. They could not well have asked me for anything more difficult. But Austrian men and women are making so splendid a fight for the cause for which Karl Marx lived and worked, that one cannot say nay to them. And so I will even try to send them a few stray, disjointed notes about my father....

To those who knew Karl Marx no legend is funnier than the common one which pictures him a morose, bitter, unbending, unapproachable man, a sort of Jupiter Tonans, ever hurling thunder, never known to smile, sitting aloof and alone in Olympus. This picture of the cheeriest, gayest soul that ever breathed, of a man brimming over with humour and good-humour, whose hearty laugh was infectious and irresistible, of the kindliest, gentlest, most sympathetic of companions, is a standing wonder—and amusement—to those who knew him.

In his home life, as in his intercourse with friends, and even with mere acquaintances, I think one might say that Karl Marx's main characteristics were his unbounded good-humour and his unlimited sympathy. His kindness and patience were really sublime. A less sweet-tempered man would have often been driven frantic by the constant interruptions, the continual demands made upon him by all sorts of people.

---

[1] These recollections by Marx's daughter, Eleanor Marx-Aveling, were published in 1895.—*Ed*.

That a refugee of the Commune—a most unmitigated old bore, by the way—who had kept Marx three mortal hours, when at last told that time was pressing, and much work still had to be done, should reply *"Mon cher Marx, je vous excuse"* is characteristic of Marx's courtesy and kindness.

As to this old bore, so to any man or woman whom he believed honest (and he gave of his precious time to not a few who sadly abused his generosity), Marx was always the most friendly and kindly of men. His power of "drawing out" people, of making them feel that he was interested in what interested them was marvellous. I have heard men of the most diverse callings and positions speak of his peculiar capacity for understanding them and their affairs. When he thought anyone really in earnest his patience was unlimited. No question was too trivial for him to answer, no argument too childish for serious discussion. His time and his vast learning were always at the service of any man or woman who seemed anxious to learn.

* * *

But it was in his intercourse with children that Marx was perhaps most charming. Surely never did children have a more delightful playfellow. My earliest recollection of him is when I was about three years old, and "Mohr" (the old home name will slip out) was carrying me on his shoulder round our small garden in Grafton Terrace, and putting convolvulus flowers in my brown curls. Mohr was admittedly a splendid horse. In earlier days—I cannot remember them, but have heard tell of them—my sisters and little brother—whose death just after my own birth was a life-long grief to my parents—would "harness" Mohr to chairs which they "mounted", and that he had to pull.... Personally—perhaps because I had no sisters of my own age—I preferred Mohr as a riding-horse. Seated on his shoulder, holding tight by his great mane of hair, then black, with but a hint of grey, I have had magnificent rides round our little garden, and over the fields—now built over—that surrounded our house in Grafton Terrace.

One word as to the name "Mohr". At home we all had nicknames (readers of *Capital* will know what a hand at giving them Marx was). "Mohr" was the regular, almost official, name by which Marx was called, not only by us, but by all the more intimate friends. But he was also our "Challey" (originally I presume a corruption of Charley!) and "Old Nick". My mother was always our "Mohme". Our dear old friend Hélène Demuth—the life-long friend of my parents, became after passing through a series of names—our "Nym". Engels, after 1870, became our "General". A very intimate friend—Lina Schöler—our "Old Mole". My sister Jenny was "Qui Qui, Emperor of China" and "Di". My sister Laura (Madame Lafargue) "the Hottentot" and "Kakadou". I was "Tussy"—a name that has remained—and "Quo Quo, Successor to the Emperor of China", and for a long time the "Getwerg Alberich" (from the *Niebelungen Lied*).

But if Mohr was an excellent horse, he had a still higher qualification. He was a unique, an unrivalled story-teller. I have heard my aunts say that as a little boy he was a terrible tyrant to his sisters, whom he would "drive" down the Markusberg at Trier full speed, as his horses, and worse, would insist on their eating the "cakes" he made with dirty dough and dirtier hands. But they stood the "driving" and ate the "cakes" without a murmur, for the sake of the stories Karl would tell them as a reward for their virtue. And so many and many a year later Marx told stories to his children. To my sisters—I was then too small—he told tales as they went for walks, and these tales were measured by miles not chapters. "Tell us another mile," was the cry of the two girls. For my own part, of the many wonderful tales Mohr told me, the most wonderful, the most delightful one, was "Hans Röckle". It went on for months and months; it was a whole series of stories. The pity no one was there to write down these tales so full of poetry, of wit, of humour! Hans Röckle himself was a Hoffmann-like magician, who kept a toyshop, and who was always "hard up". His shop was full of the most wonderful things—of wooden men and women, giants and dwarfs, kings and queens, workmen and masters, animals and birds as numerous as Noah got into the Arc, tables and chairs, carriages, boxes of all sorts and sizes. And though he was a magician, Hans could never meet his obligations either to the devil or the butcher, and was therefore—much against the grain—constantly obliged to sell his toys to the devil. These then went through wonderful adventures—always ending in a return to Hans Röckle's shop. Some of these adventures were as grim, as terrible, as any of Hoffmann's; some were comic; all were told with inexhaustible verve, wit and humour.

And Mohr would also read to his children. Thus to me, as to my sisters before me, he read the whole of Homer, the whole *Niebelungen Lied, Gudrun, Don Quixote,* the *Arabian Nights,* etc. As to Shakespeare he was the Bible of our house, seldom out of our hands or mouths. By the time I was six I knew scene upon scene of Shakespeare by heart.

On my sixth birthday Mohr presented me with my first novel—the immortal *Peter Simple*.[1] This was followed by a whole course of Marryat and Cooper. And my father actually read every one of the tales as I read them, and gravely discussed them with his little girl. And when that little girl, fired by Marryat's tales of the sea, declared she would become a "Post-Captain" (whatever that may be) and consulted her father as to whether it would not be possible for her "to dress up as a boy" and "run away to join a man-of-war" he assured her he thought it might very well be done, only they must say nothing about it to anyone until all plans were well matured. Before these plans could be matured, however, the Scott mania had set in, and the little girl heard to her horror that she herself partly belonged to the detested clan of Campbell. Then came plots for rousing the Highlands, and for reviving "the forty-five".[2] I should add that Scott was an author to whom Marx again and again returned, whom he admired and knew as well as he did Balzac and Fielding. And while he talked about these and many other books he would, all unconscious though she was of it, show his little girl where to look for all that was finest and best in the works, teach her—though she never thought she was being taught, to that she would have objected—to try and think, to try and understand for herself.

And in the same way this "bitter" and "embittered" man would talk "politics" and "religion" with the little girl. How well I remember, when I was perhaps some five or six years old, feeling certain religious qualms and (we had been to a Roman Catholic Church to hear the beautiful music) confiding

---

[1] An adventure novel by the English writer Frederick Marryat.—*Ed.*

[2] The reference is to Walter Scott's novel *Waverley* which described the events of 1745 in Scotland—an uprising against the British rule.—*Ed.*

them, of course, to Mohr, and how he quietly made everything clear and straight, so that from that hour to this no doubt could ever cross my mind again. And how I remember his telling me the story—I do not think it could ever have been so told before or since—of the carpenter whom the rich men killed....

And Marx could himself have said "suffer little children to come unto me" for wherever he went there children somehow would turn up also. If he sat on the Heath at Hampstead—a large open space in the north of London, near our old home—if he rested on a seat in one of the parks, a flock of children would soon be gathered round him on the most friendly and intimate terms with the big man with the long hair and beard, and the good brown eyes. Perfectly strange children would thus come about him, would stop him in the street.... Once, I remember, a small schoolboy of about ten, quite unceremoniously stopping the dreaded "chief of the International" in Maitland Park and asking him to "swop knives". After a little necessary explanation that "swop" was schoolboy for "exchange", the two knives were produced and compared. The boy's had only one blade; the man's had two, but these were undeniably blunt. After much discussion a bargain was struck, and the knives exchanged, the terrible "chief of the International" adding a penny in consideration of the bluntness of his blades.

How I remember, too, the infinite patience and sweetness with which, the American war[1] and Blue Books having for the time ousted Marryat and Scott, he would answer every question, and never complain of an interruption. Yet it must have been no small nuisance to have a small child chattering while he was working at his great book. But the child was never allowed to think she was in the way. At this time too, I remember, I felt absolutely convinced that Abraham Lincoln badly needed my advice as to the war, and long letters would I indite to him, all of which Mohr, of course, had to read and post. Long long years after he showed me those childish letters that he had kept because they had amused him.

And so through the years of childhood and girlhood Mohr

---

[1] *The American Civil War*—a war between the Southern and Northern States in the 1860s.—*Ed.*

was an ideal friend. At home we were all good comrades, and he always the kindest and best humoured. Even through the years of suffering when he was in constant pain, suffering from carbuncles, even to the end....

* * *

I have jotted down these few disjointed memories, but even these would be quite incomplete if I did not add a word about my mother. It is no exaggeration to say that Karl Marx could never have been what he was without Jenny von Westphalen. Never were the lives of two people—both remarkable —so at one, so complementary one of the other. Of extraordinary beauty—a beauty in which he took pleasure and pride to the end, and that had wrung admiration from men like Heine and Herwegh and Lassalle—of intellect and wit as brilliant as her beauty, Jenny von Westphalen was a woman in a million. As little boy and girl Jenny and Karl played together; as youth and maiden—he but seventeen, she twenty-one—they were betrothed, and as Jacob for Rachel he served for her seven years before they were wed. Then through all the following years of storm and stress, of exile, bitter poverty, calumny, stern struggle and strenuous battle, these two, with their faithful and trusty friend, Hélène Demuth, faced the world, never flinching, never shrinking, always at the post of duty and of danger. Truly he could say of her in Browning's words:

> Therefore she is immortally my bride,
> Chance cannot change my love nor time impair.

And I sometimes think that almost as strong a bond between them as their devotion to the cause of the workers was their immense sense of humour. Assuredly two people never enjoyed a joke more than these two. Again and again— especially if the occasion were one demanding decorum and sedateness—have I seen them laugh till tears ran down their cheeks, and even those inclined to be shocked at such awful levity could not choose but laugh with them. And how often have I seen them not daring to look at one another, each knowing that once a glance was exchanged uncontrollable laughter would result. To see these two with eyes fixed on anything but one another, for all the world like two schoolchildren, suffocating with suppressed laughter that at last despite all efforts would well forth, is a memory I would not barter for all the millions I am sometimes credited with having inherited. Yes, in spite of all the suffering, the struggles, the disappointments, they were a merry pair, and the embittered Jupiter Tonans a figment of bourgeois imagination. And if in the years of struggle there were many disillusions, if they met with strange ingratitude, they had what is given to few—true friends. Where the name of Marx is known there too is known that of Frederick Engels. And those who knew Marx in his home remember also the name of as noble a woman as ever lived, the honoured name of Hélène Demuth.

To those who are students of human nature it will not seem strange that this man, who was such a fighter, should at the same time be the kindliest and gentlest of men. They will understand that he could hate so fiercely only because he could love so profoundly; that if his trenchant pen could as surely imprison a soul in hell as Dante himself it was because he was so true and tender; that if his sarcastic humour could bite like a corrosive acid, that same humour could be as balm to those in trouble and afflicted.

My mother died in the December of 1881. Fifteen months later he who had never been divided from her in life had joined her in death. After life's fitful fever they sleep well. If she was an ideal woman, he—well, he "was a man, take him for all in all, we shall not look upon his like again".

Eleanor Marx-Aveling

FREDERICK ENGELS[1]

On November 28, 1890, Frederick Engels will be 70 years old. All socialists in the world will celebrate that birthday. On this occasion my friend Dr. Victor Adler asked me to write a short essay for the readers of the *Sozialdemokratische Monatsschrift* on the acknowledged head of the present Party.

Of all the various qualities necessary for such a difficult task I can claim only one: that I have known Engels all my life. And yet it is still questionable whether long and close intimacy enables one to portray somebody. Of all persons the most difficult to describe is oneself.

To write a biography of Marx and Engels—for the life and work of these two men are so closely associated that they cannot be separated—one would have to write not only a history of the development of socialism "from utopia to science"; one would have to write the history of the whole working-class movement over nearly half a century. For these two men were not just leaders in ideas, teachers of theory, philosophers who held themselves isolated and aloof from the working life of every day. They were always fighters, always in the front line of battle, soldiers as well as members of the General Staff of the revolution....

The details of the life of Engels are now so well known that it seems necessary only to recall them briefly. His literary and scientific works are so well known that it would be

---

[1] Published in 1890.—*Ed.*

Wilhelm Liebknecht and Tussy (Eleanor Marx)

Eleanor, Marx's youngest daughter

pretentious of me to try and give any analysis of them: here a mere chronological summary will be sufficient. But I wish to attempt a short sketch of Engels as a man and of the way he lives and works. Thus I think I shall provide pleasure for many.... For it is my opinion that the study of a life like that of Engels can only help and fire us, who are younger and are following the path he showed us.

* * *

Frederick Engels was born on November 28, 1820, at Barmen in Rhineland. His father was a manufacturer (it must not be forgotten that the Rhine provinces were then well ahead of the rest of Germany economically); his family was a very distinguished one. Probably no son born in such a family ever struck so entirely different a path from it. Frederick must have been considered by his family as the "ugly duckling". Perhaps they still do not understand that the "duckling" was in reality a "swan". One thing is clear to those who heard Engels speak about his family: he inherited his cheerful disposition from his mother.

His schooling was the usual one and he attended the Elberfeld Gymnasium for a time. At first he intended to go to university but his intention was not put into effect. A year before his final Gymnasium examination he entered a business in Barmen and then served a year as a volunteer in the army in Berlin.

In 1842 he was sent to Manchester to work in the business in which his father was a partner. He spent two years there and the importance of those two years in the classical country of capitalism, the heart of modern industry, cannot be overestimated. It was typical of him that while he was collecting material for his *Condition of the Working Class in England* he took an active part in the Chartist movement and was a regular contributor to the Chartists' *Northern Star* and Owen's *New Moral World*.

In 1844 Engels returned to Germany via Paris, where for the first time he met a man with whom he had long been corresponding and who was to become his life-long friend—Karl Marx.

The immediate fruit of this meeting was the joint publication of *The Holy Family* and the beginning of a work which was later finished in Brussels....

In the same year Engels wrote his *Condition of the Working Class in England*, a book that is still so true today, although it is forty years old, that when the English translation appeared English workers thought it had been written just a few years ago.[1] During the same period Engels wrote various essays, articles, etc.

From Paris he went back to Barmen, but only for a short time.

In 1845 he followed Marx to Brussels, where their joint work really began. Besides their enormous literary activity the two friends founded a German Workers' Society, but the most important of all was their entering the League of the Just, out of which the famous Communist League later emerged, bearing in it the kernel of the International.

Marx, still in Brussels, and Engels in Paris became in 1847 the theoretical teachers of the League of the Just and in summer the same year the first congress of the League was held in London. Engels was there as the delegate of the Paris members. The League was completely reorganised. That autumn the second congress took place, at which Marx too was present. The result of it is now known to the whole world—the *Communist Manifesto*.

From London the two friends went to Cologne and immediately plunged into practical activity. The history of this activity is recorded in the *Neue Rheinische Zeitung* and in Marx's *Revelations about the Cologne Communist Trial*.

As a result of the closing down of the newspaper and Marx's expulsion the friends were parted for a time. Marx went to Paris, Engels to Pfalz: he took part in the Baden insurrection as adjutant to Willich. He was in action three times and a long time afterwards all who saw him in battle still spoke of his extraordinary coolness and absolute scorn of danger.

In the *Neue Rheinische Zeitung. Politisch-ökonomische Revue* Engels wrote a report on the Baden insurrection. After its complete defeat he was the last to leave for Switzerland. Then he went to London, where Marx also proceeded after his expulsion from Paris.

A new period in Engels' life now began.... Marx settled

---

[1] The American edition of 1887.—*Ed.*

down in London and Engels went to Manchester to the cotton mill in which his father was a partner. There he resumed his work as a clerk.

For twenty years Engels was doomed to the forced labour of business life and for twenty years the two friends had but rare, brief, occasional meetings. But their association did not discontinue. One of my first memories is the arrival of letters from Manchester. The two friends wrote to each other almost every day, and I can remember how often Moor, as we called our father at home, used to talk to the letters as though their writer were there. "No, that's not the way it is"; "You're right there," etc., etc. But what I remember best is how Moor used sometimes to laugh over Engels' letters until tears ran down his cheeks.

In Manchester Engels was not, of course, isolated. First of all there was Wolff, "the intrepid, faithful, noble protagonist of the proletariat" to whom the first book of *Capital* is dedicated and whom we at home called *Lupus*; later came my father's and Engels' devoted friend Sam Moore (who translated *Capital* into English in collaboration with my husband), and Professor Schorlemmer, one of the most prominent chemists of today. But it is terrible to think that, apart from these friends, a man like Engels had to spend twenty years in that way. Not that he ever complained or murmured. Far from it! He was as cheerful and composed at his work as though there were nothing in the world like "going to the shop" or sitting in the office. But I was with Engels when he reached the end of this forced labour and I saw what he must have gone through all those years. I shall never forget the triumph with which he exclaimed: "For the last time!" as he put on his boots in the morning to go to the office for the last time.

A few hours later we were standing at the gate waiting for him. We saw him coming over the little field opposite the house where he lived. He was swinging his stick in the air and singing, his face beaming. Then we set the table for a celebration and drank champagne and were happy. I was then too young to understand all that and when I think of it now the tears come to my eyes.

Then in 1870 Engels came to London and immediately took upon himself a part of the abundant work that the International had undertaken. He was at the same time a member of the Executive and corresponding member for Belgium and later for Spain and Italy. Besides, Engels' literary activity was extraordinarily great and varied. From 1870 to 1880 he wrote articles and leaflets without end. But his most important work in all respects was *Herr Eugen Dühring's Revolution in Science*, which appeared in 1878. It is just as unnecessary to speak of the influence and importance of this work today as it is to speak of that of *Capital*.

During the following ten years Engels came to see my father every day; they sometimes went for a walk together but just as often they remained in my father's room, walking up and down, each on his side of the room, boring holes with his heel as he turned on it in his corner. In that room they discussed more things than the philosophy of most men can dream of. Frequently they walked up and down side by side in silence. Or again, each would talk about what was then mainly occupying him until they stood face to face and laughed aloud, admitting that they had been weighing opposite plans for the last half hour.

How much could be written about those times if space and time allowed! About the International, the Commune, and the months when our house was like a hotel where every emigrant was welcome and found help!

In 1881 my mother died, and my father, whose health was failing, did not see Engels for a few months. In 1883 he died.

Everybody knows how much Engels has done since then. He devoted most of his time to the publication of my father's works, reading proofs of new editions or supervising translations of *Capital*. I need not speak of this work or of his own original writings: only those who know Engels can appreciate the amount of work he did every day. Italians, Spaniards, Dutchmen, Danes and Rumanians (he has a thorough knowledge of all those languages), not to speak of Englishmen, Germans and Frenchmen, all come to him for help and advice.

At every difficulty that we who work in the vineyard of our master, the people, come across, we go to Engels. And never do we appeal to him in vain. The work this single man has done in recent years would have been too much for a dozen ordinary men. And Engels still works, for he knows, as we all do, that he and he alone can give to the world what Marx left behind. Engels has still a lot to do for us and he will do it!

This is a mere outline of his life. It is, so to speak, the skeleton of the man, not the man himself. To animate that skeleton one would have to be more capable than I, perhaps than any of us. We are too near him to be able to see him well.

* * *

Engels is now seventy years old. But he bears his three score and ten years with great ease. He is vigorous in body and soul. He carries his six foot odd so lightly that one would not think he is so tall. He wears a beard that grows curiously to one side and is beginning to turn grey. His hair, on the contrary, is brown without a streak of grey; at least a careful inspection was not able to detect any grey hairs. Even as far as his hair is concerned he is younger than most of us. And although Engels looks young, he is even younger than he looks. He is really the youngest man I know. As far as I can remember he has not grown any older in the last twenty hard years.

In 1869 I accompanied him to Ireland and it was very interesting to see the country with him, as he wanted to write the history of Ireland, "the Niobe[1] of the nations". Then in 1888 I accompanied him to America. In 1869 and in 1888 he was the life and soul of every party and every group in which he found himself.

On the liners *City of Berlin* and *City of New York*, he was always ready in any weather to go for a walk on deck and have a glass of lager. It seemed to be one of his unshakable principles never to go round an obstacle but always to jump or climb over it.

---

[1] *Niobe*, in Greek mythology, was the wife of Amphion, king of Thebes. She was proud of her many sons and daughters and boasted of her superiority over goddess Leto, the mother of only two children, Apollo and Artemis. As a punishment, Leto ordered Apollo and Artemis to slay all of Niobe's children and Niobe herself was changed into a rock shedding tears. Here Ireland is compared to Niobe, because she lost over 2,500,000 people as a result of hunger, ruin and emigration in the late 1840s and early 1850s.—*Ed.*

Here I must dwell for a while on one side of my father's character and of Engels' and stress it more as it is unknown to the outside world and seemingly unbelievable to most people. My father was always described as a kind of cynical, sardonic Jupiter, always ready to fulminate against friend and foe alike. But whoever looked, if only once, into his beautiful brown eyes, which were penetrating and yet at the same time so gentle, so full of humour and kindness; whoever heard his infectious, heart-warming laughter, knows that the jeering Jupiter is pure imagination. The same for Engels. There are people who represent him as an autocrat, a dictator, a carping critic. There is no truth at all in that....

I do not need to speak of Engels' inexhaustible kindness to young people: there are enough people in every country who can bear witness to it. All that I can say is that I saw him often enough put his work aside to render a friendly service to some young person and that his own work was often neglected for the sake of a beginner.

There is one thing that Engels never forgives—deceit. A man who is deceitful towards himself, and all the more towards his Party, finds no mercy with Engels. For him those are unforgivable sins....

Here I must note another feature of Engels. Although he is the most exact man in the world and has a stronger sense of duty and above all of Party discipline than anybody, he is not in the least puritanical....

Nothing besides Engels' youthful spirit and kindness is as remarkable as his versatility. He is in his element in every branch of knowledge: natural history, chemistry, botany, physics, philology ("he stutters in twenty languages," *Figaro* wrote of him in the seventies), political economy, and, last but not least, military tactics. In 1870, during the Franco-Prussian War, the articles that Engels published in *Pall Mall* made a great impression, for he foretold exactly the battle of Sedan and the shattering of the French army.

A propos, it is from that time that he was nicknamed the "General". My sister proclaimed him the "General Staff". The name stuck to him and ever since we have called him the "General". But today the name has a broader meaning: Engels is in reality the general of our working-class army....

Another feature of Engels', perhaps the most essential, must be noted. It is his absolute selflessness.

"In Marx's lifetime," he used to say, "I played second fiddle, and I think I have attained virtuosity in it and I am damned glad that I had such a good first fiddle as Marx."[1] Today Engels is the conductor of the orchestra, but he is just as modest, unpretentious and unaffected as if, as he himself said, he were "second fiddle".

I have had the opportunity, like many other people, to speak of the friendship between my father and Engels. It was one which will become as historical as that of Damon and Pythias in Greek mythology.

These notes cannot be complete without mention of two other friendships which resulted from his association with Marx and influenced his life and work.... The first is his friendship with my mother and the second, with Hélène Demuth, who died on November 4 this year and was laid to rest in the same grave as my parents.

Here is what Engels said about my mother at her graveside[2]:

"Friends!

"The noble-hearted woman whom we are burying was born in Salzwedel in 1814. Her father, the Baron of Westphalen, was sent shortly afterwards as Government Councillor to Trier and there developed a close friendship with Marx's family. The children grew up together. The two richly gifted natures found each other. When Marx went to university the community of their future life was already a settled matter.

"In 1843, after the suppression of the first *Rheinische Zeitung*, of which Marx was editor for a time, their marriage took place. Thenceforth Jenny Marx not only shared the fate, the work and the struggle of her husband, she took part in them with the greatest understanding and the most ardent passion.

"The young couple went to Paris, into a voluntary exile that only too soon became a real one. There, too, the Prus-

---

[1] Engels, Letter to Becker, October 15, 1884.—*Ed*.
[2] Eleanor Marx here quotes an article by Engels in *Der Sozialdemokrat*, "Jenny Marx, née von Westphalen". The first and last sentences are from his "Speech at the Graveside of Jenny Marx" published in *L'Egalité*.—*Ed*.

sian Government persecuted Marx. Unfortunately it must be added that a man like Alexander von Humboldt stooped so low as to take a hand in obtaining an order of expulsion against Marx. The family was forced to leave for Brussels. Then came the February Revolution. During the troubles that broke out as a result in Brussels not only Marx was arrested, but the Belgian police went so far as to throw his wife into prison without any grounds.

"The revolutionary upsurge of 1848 collapsed within the next few years. Exile again, first in Paris and then, as a result of a further intervention of the French Government, in London. And this time it was indeed a real exile with all its horrors for Jenny Marx. In spite of this, she would have overcome the material hardship which led to the death of her two boys and a little girl, but the government and the bourgeois opposition, from the vulgar liberals to the democrats, joined in a great conspiracy against her husband and showered on him the most wretched and base calumnies; the entire press united against him and deprived him of every means of defence, so that for a time he was helpless against enemies that he and she could not but despise. All this deeply wounded her. And it lasted a long time.

"But not for ever. The European proletariat again secured conditions of existence that allowed it a certain liberty of movement. The International was founded. The class struggle of the proletariat spread from country to country and her husband fought among the foremost, he was the foremost of all. Then a time began for her which compensated for some of her hardships. She lived to see the calumny which had lashed her husband dissipated like chaff before the wind; to see his teaching, which all reactionary parties, feudal as well as democratic, had exerted such great efforts to suppress, preached from the house-tops in all civilised countries and in all tongues. She lived to see the proletarian movement, which had become one with her own existence, shake the old world from Russia to America and press forward ever more confident of victory in spite of all resistance. *And one of her last joys was the striking proof of inexhaustible vitality that our German workers gave at the last Reichstag elections*.

"What this woman of such penetrating critical intellect, of such political tact, of such an energetic and passionate character and such devotedness to her comrades in the struggle did for the movement for nearly forty years has not come to the knowledge of the public or been recorded in the annals of the contemporary press. One must have lived through it. But I know this much: If the wives of the emigrants of the Commune often think of her, we others will often enough miss her keen and clever advice, keen without pretension, clever without yielding on any point of honour....

"I need not speak of her personal qualities, her friends know them and will not forget them. If there was ever a woman whose greatest happiness was to make others happy, it was this woman."

At Hélène Demuth's funeral Engels said:

"Marx often asked her advice on difficult and complicated Party matters, and, for my part, I owe all the work I have been able to do since Marx's death largely to the sunshine and help that her presence brought to my house, where she did me the honour of coming to live after Marx's death."

We alone can measure what she was to Marx and his family, and even we cannot express it in words. From 1837 to 1890 she was the true friend and helper of every one of us.

Edgar Longuet

SOME ASPECTS
OF KARL MARX'S FAMILY LIFE[1]

In sketching this outline of Karl Marx's family life I should have liked to be able to illustrate it with many personal remembrances. Unfortunately those remembrances are blurred by the years and above all by the fact that I was only three years old when I saw my grandfather for the last time.

But it is curious that among the many events that go to fill one's life certain facts remain engraved, one knows not why, in the memory.

Thus, I remember quite clearly a walk that my grandfather took my brother Jean and me for in the Bois de Champroux, which in that year 1882 still gave Argenteuil with its asparagus fields and vineyards the aspect of a remote countryside. It was during a visit Marx paid to my parents in July 1882, for since the return of my father, Charles Longuet, an ex-member of the Commune, from exile at the end of 1880, my parents lived in that country district.

I bear my grandfather no ill-will for the regrettable but, I am afraid, well-deserved, reputation that he made me during my childhood. It appears that when I was about

---

[1] These notes were written by Edgar Longuet, a member of the French Communist Party and grandson of Karl Marx (son of his daughter Jenny and Charles Longuet), in March 1949 for the 66th anniversary of Karl Marx's death and published the same year in *Cahiers du communisme*, organ of the Central Committee of the French Communist Party.—*Ed.*

eighteen months old I was very gourmand and for that reason my grandfather called me the "Wolf". Marx gave me the name because one day I was surprised biting at a raw kidney which I thought was a piece of chocolate and which I continued to devour despite my mistake.

In a letter to my mother, however, my grandfather mitigated his judgement on me: "Remember me to Jean, Harry" (my younger brother) "and the good Wolf, who is really a splendid child."

I shall come back to Marx's relations with his grandchildren later. I now want to give a brief description of his family life, without touching on his political life.

* * *

Briefly, I recall that Marx was born at Trèves in 1818, shortly after the annexation of that town by France was ended.

His father, who was of Jewish extraction and had a long line of rabbis as ancestors, had embraced the Protestant faith, which, he thought, would facilitate him his profession as lawyer.

At the age of eighteen Marx was engaged to Jenny von Westphalen, who was considered the "most beautiful girl in Trèves". Her family came from Brunswick.

I shall leave out the first part of my grandfather's life, which is well known from the political point of view, and simply recall that he arrived in Paris in 1843 and was expelled in January 1845. (It was during that stay in Paris that my mother was born, so that she was a Parisian by birth.)

He then lived in Brussels but was expelled from there too and returned to Paris on March 5, 1848, at the call of Flocon, in the name of the Provisional Government formed on February 24.

In April he left Paris and went to Germany, persuaded that the February Revolution, which had been carried out by the proletariat, had been used once more by the bourgeoisie to seize power against the working class.

In Germany he raised the standard of the revolution and fought fiercely until the day when reaction was victorious and he was again forced to go into exile.

He returned to Paris at the beginning of June 1849 and was there when the Legislative Assembly, the majority of whose members were royalists, met.

Hardly a month later he was politely given twenty-four hours to leave the city. Then, at the end of August 1849, he went to England and it was in that country, which *at that time* was the refuge for all the banished of the world, that he spent the rest of his life, thirty-four years. To start with I must recall that if, in spite of his continually declining health (liver disease, attacks of asthma, frequently repeated outbreaks of furunculosis) and of the material hardships he had to suffer, he was able to achieve what he had undertaken, it was Frederick Engels he owed it to.

The friendship of Marx and Engels deserves to go down in history like the ancient legend of Orestes and Pylades. Engels did himself violence most of his life to manage a branch of his father's business in Manchester and to ply a trade which weighed heavily upon him. His only reason for doing so was to be able to help Marx and allow him to carry out his work. There is no doubt that without Engels Marx and his family would have starved.

I wish to say a few words, too, about a second person who played an important role in Marx's life and family. I mean the excellent Hélène Demuth, familiarly called *Lenchen*.

She entered the service of my great grandmother, the Baroness von Westphalen, at the age of eight or nine and followed my grandmother everywhere, to Paris, Brussels, London, from her marriage till her death. She saw the birth and the death of the children, went with Marx's family through the horrors of poverty, hunger and distress, watched over the children, the friends and the emigrants deprived of everything, managed to feed them when everything was pawned, spent nights sewing, washing, or at their bed-side when they were ill. I have the most touching memory of her.

This admirable woman perfectly deserved to be buried with Marx, his wife and their grandson Harry in the grave at Highgate, London.

Poverty of the Emigrants in London

I should now like to give a short description of the life of an emigrant and a family of emigrants arriving in London without any resources. For Marx and his family there began a life of misery, sufferings and bereavements and I cannot give a better idea of it than by quoting a letter from Marx to Engels saying that he "could no longer bear the horrible nights that his wife spent in tears"....

In June 1850, Marx and his family, evicted from their house, took refuge in a furnished hotel in Leicester Square and later in Dean Street, where their dwelling was still very poor—a room with a small closet, so that one of the rooms was at the same time kitchen, study and drawing-room.

And the difficulties went on.

In 1851, at the birth of Franzisca, Marx wrote to Engels: "At the same time, my wife has had a child. The birth was easy, but she is still in bed for domestic reasons more than physical ones. I have literally not a farthing in the house, but I have no shortage of bills from shopkeepers, the butcher, the baker, etc....

"You will agree that all this does not make a very nice picture and that I am up to my neck in the petty-bourgeois mire. And then into the bargain I am accused of exploiting the workers and striving for a dictatorship. How horrible!..."

In a letter dated September 8, 1852, he wrote:

"My wife is ill. Jenny" (my mother) "is ill. Hélène has a sort of nervous fever. I have been and still am unable to call the doctor because I have no money to pay for medicine.

"For the past week I have been feeding my family on bread and potatoes and I wonder whether I shall manage to get some more for today."

In January 1855 a sixth child was born. They called it Tussy (my aunt Eleanor Aveling). It was so puny that it was expected to die every day. A few months later Marx had one of the greatest griefs of his life: his only boy, Edgar, his Mush, "Colonel Mush", died in his arms. The child had been struggling with death for weeks and Marx's letters had been reporting the changes for better and for worse in its condition. But in a letter on March 30 Marx wrote to Engels: "The disease has finally turned out to be phthisis of the lower abdomen, a hereditary disease in my family, and the doctors have given up all hope.... My heart is bleeding and my head on fire, although I must of course keep cool. During its illness the child has been true to itself —good and yet full of personality."

The child was indeed very intelligent and had its father's love for books.

On April 12, 1855, my poor grandfather wrote to Engels: "Our house is of course quite empty and desolate after the death of the child who was the soul of it. I cannot tell you how much we miss the boy everywhere. I have already been through all kinds of sufferings, but only now have I found out what real unhappiness is. I feel quite broken. Luckily, I have had such a headache since the day of the burial that I am no longer living.

"In the horrible sufferings that I have been through these days I have always been held up by the thought of your friendship and the conviction that we two still have an intelligent job to do on this earth."

A few weeks later, my grandmother lost her mother and inherited a few hundred thalers so that the family was able to settle in a more healthy apartment in Grafton Square.

Marx had another child who died very young. The circumstances that accompanied this death were atrocious and made such a tragic impression on my grandfather that "he was out of his wits for several days".

For many years life continued just as hard for Marx and his family except for the bereavements.

His contributions to the *New York Tribune* improved his situation a little financially for a few years, and then poverty came again, so cruel that Marx wrote to Engels that he intended to confide his children to some friends, to dismiss Hélène Demuth, to go into furnished rooms with his wife and look for employment as a common cashier.

The death of his mother brought a small inheritance in 1863. A little later his old friend Wilhelm Wolff died and left him his little fortune. This allowed Marx to clear his debts, including those contracted for the *Neue Rheinische Zeitung*, and to devote himself exclusively to scientific work as far as his health allowed. But his health did not improve and his life was several times in danger.

From then on a year seldom went by without Marx suffering from abscesses or anthraxes, added to which he had troubles caused by a liver disease.

A Prodigious Life of Work and Struggle

It would have been interesting to show how Marx, harassed by material, moral and health difficulties, succeeded in achieving such a gigantic task.

Not wishing to make these notes too long, I shall just mention at first that Marx spent whole days, from ten in the morning till seven in the evening, at the British Museum looking through Blue Books, parliamentary documents, social and economic studies, etc., and spent whole nights working at home.

He made numerous attempts to earn his living by his intellectual work but it was generally impossible for him to find publishers—besides, Engels could not countenance him wasting his time on works of secondary importance and urged him to devote every available minute to the preparation for the great work on economics that he planned. For that purpose he offered him constant help.

But that help was insufficient.

The *Neue Rheinische Zeitung* only brought Marx debts.

That was why he accepted to work for the *New York Tribune* from 1851. This obliged him to undertake numerous studies, which, however, partly fitted in with his main scientific work. Those articles were certainly valuable contributions to the general and economic history of modern times.

Unfortunately, from the financial point of view, he received payment for only one-third of those articles, the others were suppressed by the editor, who therefore did not consider himself obliged to pay for them.

Marx, it must be said, resigned himself with great misgivings to this thankless literary work that did not even allow him to feed his family.

In 1852 most of his time was taken up in connection with the arrest of the Cologne and other members of the

Communist League and the legal proceedings against them.

Marx worked untiringly with his London friends to prove that the trial was nothing but a machination of the police and the government....

Let it be recalled, finally, that it was at the very time when Marx was weighed down by hardships, that he wrote the painstaking, profound and penetrating work *The Eighteenth Brumaire.*

And all this time Marx could not leave his house because he had pawned his clothing.

The years went by, still with the same material hardships, the long days of sickness, the spells of unrelenting work, and notwithstanding everything the great work was carried on. It was the work of a fighter, a thinker, and a creator, for not limiting himself to work in his study, Marx unceasingly devoted himself to directing the International Working Men's Association as well as to his tremendous theoretical work.

In spite of everything, his house, especially when he was living in Maitland Park (which was not spared by nazi bombs), was an asylum for all emigrants and all fighters, whether English or foreign.

In my childhood I find the memory of the atmosphere that prevailed in that house where Marx lived with his wife —who, in spite of deaths and afflictions, always had a smiling welcome for her guests, most of them emigrants— and with his daughters Jenny, Laura (later the wife of Paul Lafargue) and Eleanor, the three of them remarkable for their intelligence and culture, and each deserving a separate biography.

Marx, who was worshipped by his daughters, adored children, and it is easy to imagine how terrible for him were the losses which afflicted him. Yes, Marx adored children and he was always loving and merry with them.

At the bottom of his heart this dauntless fighter had a store of sensitiveness, kindness and tender devotedness.

He would play with children as though a child himself without any thought of compromising his dignity. In the streets of his district he was known as "daddy Marx", a gentleman who always had a sweet in his pocket for the youngsters.

Karl Marx. 1882

Marx's grave in Highgate Cemetery

Later he transferred this affection to his grandchildren. "Lots of kisses to you and your little men," he wrote to my mother.

He never wrote a letter without speaking of the children: "And now give me a long account of all that Jean and the others have been doing."

In a letter written in 1881 he told my mother:

"Tussy, with the help of Engels, had just taken the case of Christmas presents for the children to the Parcel Company. Hélène asks specially to tell you that it is she who sends the frock for Harry" (he died shortly after Marx), "one for Eddy" (myself) "and a little beret for Pa" (my brother Marcel). "Laura is sending Pa a little blue suit too. From me there is a sailor suit for my dear Jean. Mama used to laugh so merrily in the very last days of her life when she told Laura how you and I went to Paris with Jean to choose a suit for him that made him look like a *'Bourgeois Gentilhomme'*."

Jean went to see him more than the rest of us because he was the eldest.

"Tell Jean," he said in another letter to my mother, "that yesterday as I was going for a walk in Maitland Park the keeper came in all his dignity to ask me about Johnny."

The expressions he used when talking about his grandchildren were often as original as they were charming:

"Lots and lots of kisses to Jean, Harry and the noble 'Wolf'. As for the 'great unknown', I cannot take such a liberty with him." (He meant my brother Marcel, who was born in April 1881 and whom he had not yet seen.)

I know no better way of showing his affection for his grandchildren than to quote the last sentence of a letter to his daughter a short time after the death of my grandmother:

"I hope to spend many a fine day with you and to fulfil worthily my duties as a grandfather."

Alas, Karl Marx was not able to put his desire into effect.

Exhausted by successive illnesses and greatly affected by the death of his wife, he had the terrible sorrow a few months later, in January 1883, of seeing his eldest daughter, my mother, Jenny Longuet, die. This last blow, on top of so many years of suffering and misery, led, on March 14,

1883, to the death of this man of genius who had consecrated his life to prepare the emancipation of the proletariat and fought till his last breath for the happiness of men.

As Frederick Engels said at his tomb:

"His name will endure through the ages, and so also will his work!"

CONFESSIONS[1]

Your favourite virtue.	Simplicity.
Your favourite virtue in man	Strength.
Your favourite virtue in woman	Weakness.
Your chief characteristic	Singleness of purpose.
Your idea of happiness	To fight.
Your idea of misery	Submission.
The vice you excuse most	Gullibility.
The vice you detest most	Servility.
Your aversion	Martin Tupper.[2]
Favourite occupation	Book-worming.
Favourite poet	Shakespeare, Aeschylus, Goethe.
Favourite prose-writer	Diderot.
Favourite hero	Spartacus, Kepler.[3]
Favourite heroine	Gretchen.[4]
Favourite flower	Daphne.
Favourite colour	Red.
Favourite name	Laura, Jenny.
Favourite dish	Fish.
Favourite maxim	*Nihil humani a me alienum puto.*
Favourite motto	*De omnibus dubitandum.*

Karl Marx

---

[1] These "Confessions" (1865) are Marx's answers to a questionnaire widespread at the time in England and Germany. Given in a semi-joking tone, these answers nevertheless are of great interest for they characterise Marx the man.—*Ed.*

[2] *Tupper, Martin* (1810-1889)—English writer, whom Marx considered the personification of vulgarity.—*Ed.*

[3] *Kepler, Johann* (1571-1630)—German astronomer who, basing himself on Copernican teachings, discovered laws of planetary movement.—*Ed.*

[4] *Gretchen*—Margaret from Goethe's *Faust*.—*Ed.*

Franzisca Kugelmann

SMALL TRAITS OF MARX'S GREAT CHARACTER[1]

When a young student, my father was an enthusiastic admirer of Karl Marx. He wrote to him, after getting his London address through Miquel, who was a member of the same students' club as he, the Normannia. To my father's immense pleasure Marx answered him, and gradually a regular correspondence was established between them. Letters were addressed to Marx under the name of A. Williams, for his correspondence was watched by the government, opened and often not forwarded. For the same reason my father was careful not to address Marx by his name in his letters but used the form of address "My esteemed and dear Friend!"

Several years later, when Marx wrote that he intended to go to the continent, my father, who in the meantime had married, invited him to be his guest and Marx accepted the invitation for a few days.

My mother, a gay young Rhineland woman, was rather worried about the visit. She expected to see a great scholar, completely absorbed with political ideas and hostile to the contemporary system of society. My father was busy the whole of the morning and part of the afternoon with his work as a doctor, how could she entertain a man like Marx? My father assured her that she would remember those days

---

[1] *Franzisca Kugelmann*—daughter of Ludwig Kugelmann, a German physician and a friend of Marx and Engels. Published here are excerpts from her reminiscences written in 1928.—*Ed.*

with pleasure for the rest of her life. Never was a prophecy more exactly fulfilled.

When the men arrived from the station, instead of the morose revolutionary she had expected my mother was greeted by a smart, good-humoured gentleman whose warm Rhenish accent at once reminded her of home. Young dark eyes smiled at her from under a mane of grey hair, his movements and his conversation were full of youthly freshness. He would not let my father make the slightest allusion to politics. He silenced him with the remark: "That is not for young ladies, we'll speak of that later." On the very first evening his conversation was so entertaining, witty and merry that the hours seemed to fly.

It happened to be the beginning of Holy Week and my parents asked Marx to go and hear Bach's Passion according to Saint Matthew with them on Good Friday. Marx refused saying that, although he was a great lover of music and particularly of Bach's, he must leave on Maundy Thursday at the latest.

However, he stayed in Hanover[1] for four weeks. It was such a pleasure for my parents to recall those days in detail with all the conversations they had with him that they were like a sunny hilltop rising above their everyday life and never shrouded in the mist of oblivion....

It was not only in our family circle that Marx was unpretentious and amiable. With my parents' acquaintances, too, he took an interest in everything and when he was particularly attracted by anybody or a witty remark was made he would adjust his monocle and survey the person in question with a friendly interest.

He was somewhat short-sighted but he wore spectacles only when he had to read or write for a long time.

My parents took particular pleasure in recalling the conversations they had with him in the early hours of the day, when they were least disturbed. My mother used even to get up earlier to finish her work about the house before breakfast. They would often sit for hours at the coffee table and my father was always sorry when he was called away by his work.

---

[1] Marx was in Hanover from April 17 to the middle of May 1867. —*Ed.*

The subjects of conversation included not only the interior and exterior life of Marx, but all fields of art, science, poetry and philosophy. Marx, who was as noble and amiable as he was great, never showed the slightest trace of pedantry. My mother took a great interest in philosophy, although she had not made a deep study of it. Marx spoke to her about Kant, Fichte and Schopenhauer and also alluded to Hegel, whose enthusiastic follower he had been in his youth. He quoted Hegel himself as having said that Rosenkranz was the only one of his students who had understood him, and incorrectly at that....

Marx had a deep hatred for sentimentality, which is but a caricature of real feeling. On occasion he would cite Goethe's words: "I have never had much of an opinion of sentimental people; if anything happens they are sure to prove bad comrades." When anybody showed exaggerated feeling in his presence he liked to recall Heine's lines:

> Ein Fraülein stand am Meere,
> Ihr war so weh und bang,
> Es grämte sie so sehre,
> Der Sonnenuntergang.[1]

Marx had known Heine and visited the unfortunate poet during his last illness in Paris. Heine's bed was being changed as Marx entered. His sufferings were so great that he could not bear to be touched, and the nurses carried him to his bed in a sheet. But Heine's wit did not forsake him and he said to Marx in a feeble voice: "See, my dear Marx, the ladies still carry me aloft."...

Marx's opinion of Heine's character was by no means a good one. He blamed him in particular for his ingratitude to friends who had helped him. For instance, the completely unjustified irony of the lines on Christiana: "For a youth so amiable no praise is too great," etc.[2]

For Marx friendship was sacred. Once a friend visiting him allowed himself the remark that Frederick Engels, being

---

[1] A girl stood by the seashore
In such great pain and dread.
What was all her grief for?
Because the sun had set.

[2] Reference is to Heine's humorous poem dedicated to Rudolph Christiana, one of his best friends.—*Ed.*

a well-to-do man, could have done more to save Marx his serious money troubles. Marx cut him short with the words: "Relations between Engels and me are so intimate and affectionate that nobody has the right to interfere." When somebody said a thing that displeased him he generally answered with a joke. In general he never resorted to coarse means of defence but retaliated with sharp thrusts which never missed their mark.

There was probably no field of science into which he had not penetrated deeply, no art for which he was not an enthusiast, no beauty of nature which did not arouse his admiration. But he could not bear truthlessness, hollowness, boasting or pretence.

For about an hour and a half before lunch he would write letters, work or read newspapers in the room that he had at his disposal besides his bedroom. It was there too that he looked through the first volume of *Capital*. There was a statue of Minerva Medica with her symbolical little owl. Marx, who had a great admiration for my mother, her kindheartedness, ready wit and good humour and her knowledge, which was extensive for her age, particularly in the fields of poetry and literature, once said to her jokingly that she was a young goddess of wisdom herself. "No, I am not," my mother answered, "I am only the little screech-owl that sits listening at her feet." That was why he sometimes called her his dear little owl, a name which he later gave to a little girl whom he loved very much and who used to sit on his knee for hours playing and chatting with him.

He used to call my mother "Madame la Comtesse" because of her self-assurance in society and because she attached great importance to good manners. Soon he never gave her any other name, no matter who happened to be present.

It was a habit in the Marx family to give nicknames to people. He himself was called Moor, by his daughters as well as by his friends. His second daughter Laura, Mrs. Lafargue, was generally called "das Laura" or Master Kakadou, after a fashionable tailor in an old novel, because of the exceptional taste and smartness with which she dressed. Marx called his eldest daughter Jenny "Jennychen". My mother also mentioned her nickname but I have forgotten what it was. Eleanor, the youngest daughter, was always called "Tussy".

He gave my father the name Wenzel. The reason was that my father once said that a guide in Prague had bored him with details about two Bohemian rulers, the good Wenzel and the bad one. The bad one had St. John Nepomucen thrown into the Moldau, the good one was very pious.[1] My father was very outspoken in his sympathies and antipathies and Marx would call him the good or the bad Wenzel according to his attitude. Later he also sent him his photo dedicated to "his Wenzel".

He often gave my parents' friends and acquaintances other names in their absence and said they should be their real names, although he often chose names that were not very typical but common ones. As a result, every time Marx was introduced to any of our acquaintances my father would afterwards ask: "Well, Marx, what should their name really be?..."

He was always merry, ready to joke and tease, and he was never more bored than when someone tactlessly asked him about his doctrine. He never answered such questions. In the family he called this curiosity about him "travelling opinion". But it was a rare occurrence.

Once a gentleman asked him who would clean shoes in the future state. He answered vexedly, "You should." The tactless questioner understood and was silent. That was perhaps the only time that Marx lost his temper....

Party comrades from everywhere, often from the most distant parts, came to visit Marx. He received them all in his room. Long conversations on politics often ensued and they were continued in my father's study....

Marx's taste was most refined in poetry as well as in science and the imitative arts. He was extraordinarily well-read and had a remarkable memory. He shared my father's enthusiasm for the great poets of classical Greece, Shakespeare and Goethe; Chamisso and Rückert[2] were also among his favourites. He would quote Chamisso's touching poetry *The Beggar and His Dog*. He admired Rückert's art in writ-

---

[1] The allusion is to the Czech Prince Saint Wenzel (circa 908-929) and the Czech King Wenzel IV (1361-1419) who had John of Nepomucen executed.—*Ed.*

[2] *Chamisso, Adelbert* (1781-1838)—German romantic poet, fought feudal reaction. *Rückert, Friedrich* (1788-1866)—German romantic poet and translator of oriental poetry.—*Ed.*

ing and especially his masterly translation of Hariri's *Maqāmas*, which are incomparable in their originality. Years later Marx presented it to my mother in remembrance of that time.

Marx was remarkably gifted for languages. Besides English, he knew French so well that he himself translated *Capital* into French,[1] and his knowledge of Greek, Latin, Spanish and Russian was so good that he could translate from them at sight. He learned Russian by himself "as a diversion" when he was suffering from carbuncles.

He was of the opinion that Turgenev[2] wonderfully renders the peculiarities of the Russian soul in its veiled Slavonic sensitivity. Lermontov's[3] descriptions, he thought, were hardly to be excelled and seldom equalled.

His favourite among the Spaniards was Calderon.[4] He had several of his works with him and often read us parts of them....

In our flat there was a large room with five windows which we called the hall and where we used to play music. Friends of the house called it Olympus because of the busts of Greek gods around the walls. Throned above them all was Zeus Otricolus.

My father thought Marx greatly resembled the last mentioned and many people agreed with him. Both had a powerful head with abundant hair, a magnificent thoughtful brow, an authoritative and yet kind expression. Marx's calm yet warm and lively nature, knowing no absent-mindedness or excitement, my father thought, also made him resemble his Olympian favourites. He liked to quote Marx's pertinent answer to the reproach that "the gods of the classics are eternal rest without any passions". On the contrary, Marx said, they were eternal passion without any unrest. My father could get very irritated when expressing his opinion of those who tried to drag Marx into the agitation of their political party undertakings. He wanted Marx, like the Olympian father of the gods and of men, only to flash

---

[1] Marx did not translate Book I of *Capital* into French, but carefully edited J. Roy's translation with which he was not satisfied.—*Ed.*

[2] *Turgenev, Ivan Sergeyevich* (1818-1883)—great Russian writer.—*Ed.*

[3] *Lermontov, Mikhail Yuryevich* (1814-1841)—great Russian poet.—*Ed.*

[4] *Calderon, Pedro* (1600-1681)—prominent Spanish playwright.—*Ed.*

his lightning into the world and occasionally hurl his thunder against it but not to waste his precious time in everyday agitation. The days thus flowed quickly by, filled with serious or merry conversation. Marx himself often called that period an oasis in the desert of his life.

Two years later my parents again had the pleasure of entertaining Marx for a few weeks, this time with his eldest daughter Jenny. The latter, an attractive slender girl with dark curly hair, greatly resembled her father in nature and appearance. She was merry, lively and amiable and most refined and tactful in her manners; she hated anything noisy and showy.

My mother quickly made friends with her and maintained her affection for her as long as she lived. She often said how well-read Jenny was, how broadminded and how enthusiastic for all that was noble and beautiful. She was a great admirer of Shakespeare and must have possessed dramatic talent, for she once played Lady Macbeth in a London theatre. Once at our house, but only in the presence of my parents and her father, she played that role in the diabolical scene of the letter. With the money that she earned on the occasion mentioned in London she bought a velvet coat for the faithful maid who had left Trier with the family for England and in joys, sorrows and privations remained firm in her love and attachment to them.

None of the Marx family had the gift of being economical or practical in money affairs. Jenny related that when, shortly after her marriage, her mother inherited a small sum, the young couple had it paid out to them entirely, and put it in a little chest with two handles. They had it in the coach with them and during their wedding journey they took it to the different hotels at which they stayed. When they had visits from friends or fellow-thinkers in need they put the chest open on the table in their room and any one could take as much as he pleased. Needless to say it was soon empty. They later suffered frequent and bitter want in London. Marx related how they were obliged to pawn or sell everything valuable that they had. The von Westphalen family were distant relations to the family of the Dukes of Argyll. When Jenny von Westphalen married Marx, her dowry included silver bearing the arms of the Argylls which had been in the family for a long time. Marx himself took a few heavy silver spoons to the pawnshop and was immediately asked to explain how those objects with the well-known crest came into his possession. This of course he easily did. When his only son died, their need was so great that they were unable to pay the burial expenses.... Marx's hair went grey that night....

During her stay in Hanover, Jenny made my mother a present of what was called a *Confession Book*. They were then the fashion in England and later they appeared in Germany under the name *Erkenne Dich Selbst*.[1] Marx was to be the first to write in it, and Jenny wrote the prescribed questions for him on the first page. But they are still unanswered.[2] Jenny wrote on the second page and my parents found the confession so characteristic of her and her peculiar nature that I shall copy it.

She wrote it in English, being better able to write that language than German. She said she could write as much on one page in English as on four in German, English being briefer, more precise and to the point. She wrote her intimate letters in French, which she considered warmer and more suitable to express thoughts and feelings. In German her pronunciation was pure Rhinelandish, like that of her father. She had never lived in the Rhine province but she had always heard that accent from her childhood in the speech of her parents and the faithful maid from Trier.

A few explanations are necessary to understand the confession. Jenny says that her favourite virtue in woman is devotion. The conversation on the evening on which she wrote it had been about religion. Marx, Jenny and my father were freethinkers whereas my mother, although disliking any kind of bigotism or dogmatic narrow-mindedness, was of a different opinion.... My mother spoke so simply, profoundly and sincerely and without any sentimentality that everybody was moved. It was remembering this that Jenny wrote that her favourite virtue in woman was devotion.

Both father and daughter hated Napoleon I, whom they simply called Bonaparte, but they despised Napoleon III so much that they never even pronounced his name. That

---

[1] Know yourself.—*Tr.*
[2] Marx's answers to similar questions are given on page 179 of the present collection.—*Ed.*

is why Jenny wrote that the historical characters she disliked most were "Bonaparte and his nephew"....

Jenny shared her father's enthusiasm for classical music. She thought Händel's works definitely revolutionary. She did not yet know Wagner: she heard *Tannhäuser* for the first time in Hanover, excellently performed, and was so delighted with it that she included Wagner in her favourite composers. Her maxim in the confession seems to be a quotation, being given in quotation marks. She did not fill in her idea of happiness and misery. I shall not translate, but shall just copy the original.

My favourite virtue	Humanity.
My favourite quality of man	Moral courage.
My favourite quality of woman	Devotion.
Ideal of happiness	
Ideal of misery	
The vice I excuse	Prodigality.
The vice I detest	Envy.
My aversion	Knights, priests, soldiers.
Favourite occupation	Reading.
Characters of history I most dislike	Bonaparte and his nephew.
Favourite poet	Shakespeare.
Favourite prose-writer	Cervantes.
Favourite composer	Händel, Beethoven, Wagner.
Favourite colour	Red.
Favourite maxim	"To thine own self be true."[1]
Favourite motto	*Alle für Einen, Einer für Alle.*[2]

When we had company, Joseph Rissé, an excellent concert singer, used sometimes to sing. He had a baritone voice of remarkable power and scale and was very talented. Among

---

[1] Shakespeare, *Hamlet.—Ed.*
[2] All for one and one for all.—*Tr.*

other things he published a collection of Irish folk songs by Thomas Moore[1] in his own translation and musical adaptation under the title *Erin's Harp*. One book was dedicated to my father. Marx, like the whole of his family, had great sympathy for unfortunate oppressed Ireland and loved to listen to these moving songs. Tussy manifested her sympathy for Ireland by making green her favourite colour and dressing mostly in green.

O'Donovan Rossa, an Irish freedom fighter, was put in prison and odiously treated by the English. Jenny, who had never seen him, wrote to him under her pen-name, J. Williams, full of admiration for his steadfastness. Mrs. Rossa, hearing that the writer of the letters was a girl, is said to have been extremely jealous. This greatly amused Marx....

Party friends often came to see Marx during this period. One of them was Herr Dietzgen,[2] a calm, distinguished man whom Marx and Jenny held in high esteem. It was his quiet way accompanied by a great capacity for work and action that inspired their sympathy....

One day a visitor behaved in a rather obstinate and autocratic way. "To hear him," Marx said, "you wonder why nobles are not worse than they are, considering their education and surroundings...."

He never violently or insultingly manifested his displeasure during a conversation.

He would unhorse his opponent, as in a tournament, but he never knocked him down....

* * *

Marx and Jenny's long stay with us naturally led to lively correspondence when they returned to London.

It has already been mentioned that Jenny preferred to use French for letter-writing and English for brief notes. Eleanor always wrote in English, Marx and his wife in German. Mrs. Marx wrote perfectly charming letters giving not only a vivid description of her life but even mentioning details about the life of my parents that showed how

---

[1] *Moore, Thomas* (1779-1852)—English romantic poet, Irish by birth; wrote a number of poems on the national liberation struggle of the Irish people.—*Ed.*

[2] *Dietzgen, Joseph* (1828-1888)—German leather worker, socialist; self-taught philosopher who independently arrived at dialectical materialism.—*Ed.*

well she had got to know them from what her husband and Jenny told her and what cordial interest she took in all that concerned us. My mother could read and speak both French and English, but her mother tongue came more naturally and fluently in correspondence....

For Christmas the whole of the Marx family sent us fondly chosen keep-sakes and pretty pieces of needlework. One was a silk theatre hat of their own making decorated with flowers. It could not be worn in Germany but my mother kept it for a long time as a souvenir. Several times they sent us a huge home-made plum-pudding....

In order to see Marx again and make acquaintance with Mrs. Marx and the Lafargues my father overcame his dislike for occasions and meetings of the sort and went to The Hague to the Congress of the Social-Democrats.[1]

My father described Mrs. Lafargue as a beautiful, elegant and amiable woman. Mrs. Marx, slim and young-looking, he said, took a passionate interest in Party life and seemed to have given herself up to it entirely....

A few years later my parents met Marx and Eleanor in Karlsbad, thus making personal acquaintance with the latter, with whom they had often chatted by letter. Jenny was already Mrs. Longuet and could not leave her husband and child.

Eleanor—Tussy as they called her—was very much unlike her elder sister both in character and figure. Her features were not so fine, but she too had her father's intelligent brown eyes. Although she was not beautiful she was certainly attractive. She had beautiful dark blond hair with a golden shimmer....

My mother had the impression that the youngest daughter, being the pet of the family, was spoilt by everybody and followed all her caprices like a pampered child. She worshipped her father just as Jenny did. She was very intelligent and warm-hearted and so boundlessly frank that she told everybody what she thought without any ceremony whether it pleased them or not....

Marx was the same as before—unchanged even in his appearance. He watched with interest the international life

---

[1] The Hague Congress of the First International in September 1872.—*Ed.*

of the health-resort and conferred the usual witty nicknames on a few of the more conspicuous passers-by.

He was delighted at the various beautiful walks in the wooded mountains, especially the romantic Egertal. Legend has personified some curiously shaped rocks there and given them the name of Hans Heiling's Rocks.

Hans Heiling is related to have been a young shepherd who won the heart of the beautiful nymph Eger. She demanded eternal faithfulness under pain of terrible vengeance. Hans Heiling swore never to abandon her, but after a few years he violated his vow and married a girl from the village. The wrathful nymph suddenly appeared out of the river at the wedding and turned the whole company into stone.

Marx took pleasure in looking for the figures of the musicians walking at the head of the wedding cortège with their horns and trumpets, the bride's coach and a festively attired old woman gathering her skirts together to step into the coach. At the same time he would listen to the quick-flowing seething river whose gurgling in the magic valley was supposed to represent an immortal being ever weeping over the fickleness of man.

In Dallwitz we visited the Oaks of Körner,[1] under which the famous poet often spent his time while recovering from serious wounds and composed the beautiful poem *The Oaks*.

Marx greatly enjoyed a visit to the Aich porcelain works where he watched porcelain being made....

Marx took pleasure in listening to the excellent resort orchestra which was conducted by Master Labitsky. As for serious talks on politics or discussion of Party affairs, he confined them to an absolute minimum during the short morning walk he had with my father or other men of his acquaintance. Among the latter was a Polish revolutionary, Count Plater, who was so taken up with his ideas that he obviously found it difficult to take part in a light conversation, which was what Marx insisted upon in broader society or in the pleasant company of ladies. The Count was under average height, black-haired and somewhat clumsy. The historical artist Otto Knille, a friend of my father's, was of the opinion that if anybody was asked which of the two

---
[1] *Körner, Theodor* (1791-1813)—German romantic poet, participant in the liberation war against Napoleon.—*Ed.*

was the count, Marx or Plater, the answer would certainly be the former. Marx liked frequent conversations on art with Knille. Thus the days went by in a variety of pleasant occupations.

Suddenly, during a long walk Marx and my father had together towards the end of our stay, a difference occurred between them which was never smoothed down. My father only made vague allusions to it. It seems that he tried to persuade Marx to refrain from all political propaganda and complete the third book of *Capital* before anything else.... "Marx was a hundred years ahead of his time," he often said later, "but they are more likely to have immediate success who are in step with their time: those who look too far ahead miss things near at hand which shorter-sighted people see more clearly."

Perhaps my father was over-zealous at the time, rather like the "bad Wenzel". This Marx could not countenance in a man so much younger than he and took for an encroachment upon his freedom. As a result their correspondence broke off. Tussy indeed wrote now and again but I do not know whether Jenny did. Tussy always gave wishes from her father, who also sent my mother books in memory of earlier talks together: Rückert's translation of Hariri's *Maqãmas*, Chamisso's works, and E.T.A. Hoffmann's *Klein Zaches*. This satire in the form of a legend particularly amused Marx. He himself never wrote any more. He probably did not intend to hurt my father by ignoring him and yet he could not forget the past.

My father never got over the pain that the break with a friend whom he still respected to the same degree caused him. However, he never made any attempt at a reconciliation, for he could not go back on his conviction. After Marx's death my mother seldom received letters from Tussy....

The association between my parents and Marx, whom they held so dear that they always lovingly remembered every detail of it, can be described in the words of Schiller:

> Unaufhaltsam enteilet die Zeit—Sie sucht das Beständige;
> Sei getreu, und Du legst ewige Fesseln ihr an."[1]

---

[1] Time hurries without tarrying, seeking what is permanent. Be faithful, and you will enchain her for ever.—*Tr.*

N. Morozov

VISITS TO KARL MARX[1]

In December 1880 I made a trip to London and went to see Marx with Lev Hartmann, one of my Narodnaya Volya[2] comrades who had often been at Marx's. We went by the London Metropolitan Railway, which was then powered by steam-engines. Marx was alone with his daughter Eleanor at the time.

"Mr. Marx in?" Hartmann asked the young maid when she opened the door in response to his three knocks.

She recognised him and answered that Marx was still at the British Museum, but that his daughter was in.

Almost immediately on our entry into the parlour, his daughter, a slim attractive girl of the German type, came in. She reminded me of the romantic Gretchen, or Margaret, in *Faust*.

Our conversation started in English, but noticing that I had difficulty over some English word and used a French

---

[1] *Morozov, Nikolai Alexandrovich* (1854-1946)—active figure in the Russian revolutionary movement, Narodnik; chemist and astronomer, honorary member of the U.S.S.R. Academy of Sciences. His reminiscences of Marx were published in 1935.—*Ed.*

[2] *Narodnaya Volya* (People's Will)—a secret political organisation of the revolutionary-minded intelligentsia—Narodniks—founded in 1879. Adopting the stand of Narodnik utopian socialism, they embarked on the road of political struggle believing the overthrow of the autocracy and conquest of political power to be the most important task. Members of the Narodnaya Volya resorted to individual terrorism in their fight against the tsarist autocracy. After the assassination of Tsar Alexander II (March 1, 1881) by them, the tsarist government smashed the organisation and by the latter half of the 1880s it ceased to exist.—*Ed.*

one instead, Eleanor immediately switched over to French, and we continued in that language.

She repeated that her father was at the British Museum and would not come home till evening. We went away after half an hour and returned at the agreed time next day.

I remember quite well that my first impression on seeing Marx was: How like his portrait he is! After the first introductions we sat down at a small table on a couch against the wall and I laughed as I told Marx my impression of him. He also laughed and said he was often told that and that it was rather a curious feeling to be like one's portrait instead of one's portrait being like oneself.

He seemed to me to be of rather medium stature but of broad build. He was most affable to us both. One at once felt in all his motions and words that he fully understood his outstanding importance. I did not notice in him any of the moroseness or unapproachableness that somebody had spoken to me about. There was a fog in London at the time and lamps were lit in all the houses. The lamp at Marx's, I distinctly remember, had a green shade. But even by that light I could see him and his study quite well. Three of the walls were lined with books and there were portraits on the fourth.

Nobody except Eleanor came into the room and I formed the impression that there were no other members of the family at home. Eleanor kept running in and taking part in the conversation, sitting a little aside on the couch. She also brought us tea and biscuits.

The conversation was mainly on Narodnaya Volya matters, in which Marx showed a great interest. He said that he, like all other Europeans, imagined our struggle with the autocracy as something fabulous, like a fantastic novel.

I went to see Marx two days later, before leaving London, and again spent a while with him and his daughter. When I said good-bye he gave me five or six books which he had ready for me. He also promised to write a foreword to the one we chose to be printed as soon as we sent him the first proofs of our translation.

When he heard that I was going back to Russia in two or three weeks he heartily shook hands with me and wished me a happy return from Russia. We both promised to write but our promise did not materialise. On my return to Geneva I found a letter from Perovskaya[1] telling me that a number of events that were being prepared demanded my prompt return. I packed my things and left, but on February 28, as I was crossing the frontier under the name of Lockier, a student of Geneva University, I was arrested and taken to the Warsaw citadel. There I learned of the events of March 1[2] from Tadeusz Balicki, a comrade who was in the cell next to mine and tapped the information on the wall.

I was imprisoned first in the Alexeyevsky Ravelin, Peter and Paul Fortress, and then in Schlisselburg. Until my release in 1905 I did not know the outcome of my conversation with Marx. In fact I did not really know until 1930, when, in a publication of the political convicts' society, *Literature of the "Narodnaya Volya" Party*, I suddenly saw Marx's Preface to the *Communist Manifesto* published by the "Social Revolutionary Library" to the foundation of which I had contributed. That awoke in me many reminiscences.

I remembered my visits to Marx and his daughter; how, leaving Geneva in haste for Russia, I gave one of the "Social Revolutionary Library" workers who were remaining (I think it was Plekhanov) Marx's *Manifesto* and the other books to be translated into Russian.

It caused me particular joy to read in the Preface by Marx which I have just mentioned the words:

"The tsar was proclaimed the chief of European reaction. Today[3] he is a prisoner of war of the revolution, in Gatchina, and Russia forms the vanguard of revolutionary action in Europe."

---

[1] *Perovskaya, Sophia Lvovna* (1853-1881)—Russian revolutionary, prominent member of the Narodnaya Volya; executed by the tsarist government.—*Ed.*
[2] On March 1, 1881, Tsar Alexander II was killed by members of the Narodnaya Volya.—*Ed.*
[3] In 1881. (*Note by Morozov.—Ed.*)

Edward Aveling, Dr. Sc.

ENGELS AT HOME[1]

1

The newspapers, socialist and otherwise, all over the world have given an account of the life and works of the great socialist who has just died. In this article something will be said of the inner side of his life.

The most impressive personalities I have ever met were Karl Marx, Charles Darwin, Frederick Engels, and, in quite another direction of life, Henry Irving.[2] In all four cases great intellectual power was combined with great physical qualities. In the two cases of Marx and Darwin, although their works, written and active, have been more or less known to me, I had the great privilege of meeting them in the flesh on only one or two occasions. The only time that I saw Marx alive was when, as a young man, I gave a lecture to the children of the Orphan Working School, Haverstock Hill, on "Insects and Flowers". It was a fête day at the school, and, besides the children, there was an audience of people interested in the school. When the lecture was over, an old gentleman with a very leonine head, together with a lady and a young girl, came up and introduced themselves to me. The gentleman was Karl Marx, the lady his wife, Jenny von Westphalen, and the young girl their daughter Eleanor. I remember to this day the kind and generous words of too generous appreciation and encouragement that Marx

---

[1] *Aveling, Edward* (1851-1898)—English socialist, writer, husband of Eleanor Marx. Reminiscences were published in 1895.—*Ed.*

[2] *Irving, Henry* (1838-1905)—well-known English producer and actor; played in Shakespeare's tragedies.—*Ed.*

said to me. The next time I saw him he was dead. But I have still the impression of great bodily strength that he made upon me....

Engels was just upon six feet in height, and, until his last illness, an erect, soldierly man, bearing his burden of over seventy years lightly. This military bearing, with the quick, springy step, had some relation with the name by which he was always known to his intimate friends—the "General". The actual origin of the name was his remarkable letters to the *Pall Mall Gazette* during the Franco-German War in 1870. In one of these he prophesied, some eight days before September 2, the decisive victory of the Germans over the French at Sedan. The letters altogether showed such a knowledge of the art of war that the public believed they were written by a great military authority. As indeed they were. But the great military authority was the Manchester cotton-spinner and socialist. Of course, the name had later on also the inner significance that he was the leader in the fight of the socialist army against capitalism, after the death of the commander-in-chief, Marx.

2

Who that was present, only once even, will ever forget those wonderful Sundays at 122, Regent's Park Road! The friend of Marx and his wife and of Engels, Hélène Demuth, was alive and acting as his housekeeper and as his trusted counsellor and adviser, not only in the matters of daily life, but even in politics, where her shrewd common sense, transparent honesty, and judgment of men, women, and things, made her a helpmate even to the two giants Marx and Engels....

It was a little like the Tower of Babel business. For not only those of us that were really of his family were present, but the socialists from other countries made 122, Regent's Park Road their Mecca.

Engels could converse with all of them in their own language. Like Marx, he spoke and wrote German, French, and English perfectly; nearly as perfectly Italian, Spanish, Danish; and also read, and could get along with, Russian, Polish, and Rumanian, not to mention such trivialities as Latin and Greek.

Every day, every post, brought to his house newspapers and letters in every European language, and it was astonishing how he found time, with all his other work, to look through, keep in order, and remember the chief contents of them all. When anything of his writings, or of Marx's writings, was to be translated into other languages, the translators always sent the translations to him for supervision and correction. And who shall say there is nothing in phrenology, when it is recorded that a phrenologist at Yarmouth, examining Engels' head for bumps, said, to the huge delight of his companions, that the gentleman was a "good man of business" (which was true enough), "but had no talent for languages" (which was not strictly true).

Besides his language qualifications, Engels was in all other respects an admirable host. He was hospitality itself, and of very good breeding.... During the week days, unless some of us went over to see him, and lunch or dine, he lived with singular frugality. But on the Sundays, with his friends around him, his delight in seeing them enjoying themselves with the best of everything he could provide was itself a delight....

Stepnyak[1] came occasionally, and Vera Zasulich,[2] since she came to England, was one of the constant visitors that needed no invitation. Georgy Plekhanov, her faithful friend and fellow-worker, one of the most able thinkers and wittiest men in the Party, whom the anarchists dread more than perhaps any other living writer, was, of course, during his short stay in England, always at Engels'....

There was another foreign American whom the Atlantic kept away from Engels' house, but who was one of his most welcome and constant correspondents, one who was, perhaps, of all men the closest intimate in the later years of both Marx and Engels. His name is Friedrich Adolf Sorge of Hoboken, near New York. Our meeting and association with him is amongst the most beautiful memories of the journey that my wife and I made with Engels and that prince of

---

[1] *Stepnyak*—pen-name of *Kravchinsky, Sergei Mikhailovich* (1851-1895)—Russian publicist and writer, prominent figure in the revolutionary Narodnik movement of the 1870s.—*Ed.*

[2] *Zasulich, Vera Ivanovna* (1849-1919)—prominent figure in the Narodnik and the Social-Democratic movement.—*Ed.*

chemists, socialists, and good fellows, the late Professor Schorlemmer, in 1888....

Naturally, here, there is no need to mention in detail those, like the daughters of Marx, their husbands, Paul Lafargue and the present writer, Sam Moore, a very old, tried, and trusty friend of both the authors of the *Communist Manifesto*, and Karl Schorlemmer.

Time and space would fail me to speak of all the casual socialists, if I may call them so, who, on flying visits to England, went to see Engels. And it must be borne in mind that he received not only the more prominent men and women; every soldier in the army was welcome at the "General's".

At the same time we must not think that his hospitality or friendship was, in any sense at all, general. He would not receive, and did not receive any whom he mistrusted. On one occasion at least, I remember when someone had come in with a deputation of foreigners, Engels made no bones whatever about instantly having him shown off the premises....

3

I think there is scarcely one of those I have mentioned who would not say with me that Engels was one of the most helpful men in the world. His very presence was an inspiration. So was his indomitable courage and hopefulness. When some of the younger were for despairing and giving way, this unconquerable fighter never lost heart, although he gave it again and again to the weaker ones. For those of us who saw him every Sunday of our lives of late years, and very often several times in the week, I may say that the loss of him is quite irreparable.

In all difficulties of every kind he was the man to be consulted—his was the advice to be followed. His encyclopaedic knowledge was always at the service of his friends. Everyone who had some special subject of his own found that Engels knew it better than himself. Thus, as to natural science, no matter what branch of it or what part of that branch he was asked about, he was always able to give some new idea, some further help.

As to politics, the one subject that all his friends had in common, all of them went to him for guidance. He knew not only the general principles, but the most minute details, of the economic, historical, political movement in every country.

His knowledge of the English movement, e.g., was extraordinarily profound and acute. It is something for the English to remember that he was upon the international platform of the Legal Eight Hours Demonstration Committee at every demonstration from the first in 1890 until in 1895 his failing health prevented him from coming.

To the last he kept up his interests in and study of contemporary politics. His acute criticisms upon the war between China and Japan[1] were as far-seeing as all of the many we have heard him make upon the events of the past few years. These were criticisms that simply astounded one by their profundity and astonishing grasp of everything and the bearing of everything, and that when they cautiously took the shape of prophecy upon political events were singularly accurate.

The very last political talk that he had was with the wife of the present writer, when she came back from Nottingham upon July 28th (he died on August 5th), and told him of the Independent Labour Party movement there. He was then far past speaking, but he kept up an energetic and most interested conversation upon the matter, asking pertinent and searching questions by the aid of his slate and pencil.

Engels was a good hater, as, indeed, everyone must be who is a good lover. He had at times, when he felt something wrong had been done, outbursts of anger; but he generally "did well to be angry".

Oddly as it may sound, in some things he was conservative. He was a man of habit. He liked certain things done at the same time and in the same way each day.

But there are no words to speak of his reliability, his integrity, the strict business habits, and accuracy, which he seemed, in the best sense, to carry into his political and social relations. As Vera Zasulich said the other day, many a time he kept some of us from doing and saying the wrong thing by our thought—what would the General think of this?

---

[1] In 1894-95.—*Ed.*

It is difficult to conceive a more clear and luminous intellect. Whatever subject he touched he threw a flood of light upon. You saw what you had not seen before, and you saw more accurately that which you had seen. *Nihil tetigit quod non ornavit*, wrote Johnson of Oliver Goldsmith.[1] His friends may write of Engels, "he touched nothing that he did not throw light upon." And his style as a writer, both in German and English, was what is especially rare in a German, lucid, bright, and trenchant.

4

With all these remarkable qualities, he had the rare and saving grace of humour. He enjoyed a joke in every language. He was the most jovial of companions. Upon those immortal Sundays necessarily most of the talk ran upon political and Party matters. We had all come to learn something. But much of the talk was of the lightest nature, and the fun was sometimes fast and furious.

When there were only a few of us there, he loved a game of cards for counters at the high price of a halfpenny a dozen, and was as keen about making "matrimony" or "nap" as if the fate of nations depended upon it....

Our field nights were those of the German elections. Then Engels laid in a huge cask of special German beer, laid on a special supper, invited his very intimates. Then, as the telegrams came pouring in from all parts of Germany far on into the night, every telegram was torn open, its contents read aloud by the General, and if it was victory we drank, and if it was defeat we drank.

In 1888, as I have said, we had a journey with him and Schorlemmer to America and Canada. Engels was the youngest of the party. He preferred, on board ship, leaping over a seat to walking round it. He never once, like the ordinary traveller, got out of temper, except when he counted sixty-eight mosquito bites before breakfast (his breakfast), and when our luggage was at New York and we were at Boston....

---

[1] *Goldsmith, Oliver* (1728-1774)—English writer, prominent representative of bourgeois Enlightenment in England.—*Ed*.

During his last illness at Eastbourne, in spite of all the pain and weakness, there were flashes of the old geniality and joviality, and never, to the very end, did his kindness to and thoughtfulness for everyone for a moment cease. Of that kindness and generosity this is not the place to speak. Every one of his friends can think of that unparalleled generosity and kindness silently, and will have much food for thought....

Engels was an atheist. That is, he was absolutely without God, and therefore with hope in the world....

His life was a beautiful one, and he loved it.... With his knowledge, his good work well done, his certainty of the future of the movement, his troops of friends—among whom of course Marx was the first, the last, the be-all and the end-all—his intense joy of living, he, more than most men, rightly enough loved and clung to life. Not, of course, that he had for a moment the slightest fear of death....

It is something for English people to remember that the work of Marx and Engels was mainly done for the world in this little country, and that both of them died here. That is a higher honour than can be conferred by the tombs and mausoleums of all the kings and conquerors in the world. The places for the dead that will be most visited hereafter will be the grave at Highgate, and the simple little building among the pines of Woking.[1]

---

[1] *Highgate*—cemetery in London where Marx is buried. In *Woking*, near London, there is a crematory where Engels' body was cremated.—*Ed.*

Fanni Kravchinskaya

REMINISCENCES

Plekhanov knew Sergei Mikhailovich[1] and kept up correspondence with him. Sergei Mikhailovich once got a letter from him in which, among other things, he wrote: "You are living in London. What are you doing there? Do you know that Engels lives there? It is not often that such men are born. That is why I insist that you make his acquaintance and send me an account. It is outrageous that you have not yet been to see him. You absolutely must go."

Engels lived in a large house which was open of a Sunday to those who wished to see him. You could meet him in his large hall every Sunday surrounded by socialists, critics and writers. Anybody who wanted to see Engels could just go.

One Sunday my husband and I went to Engels' with Marx's daughter Eleanor.

The charming old man made the most favourable impression on me. I was very shy, and to my discomfort he gave me a seat quite near him. I kept drawing nearer to Marx's daughter and avoided talking to Engels, but he, like the courteous man that he was, naturally started to entertain me. I could not speak any foreign languages and therefore had but one wish—to be left in peace. Engels spoke French, German and English. The conversation was on all possible subjects, mainly political. There were arguments.

His housekeeper sat as usual at the opposite end of the table. All that she did was to give every new arrival a fairly "liberal" helping of meat and salad and keep the glasses full of wine.

---
[1] S. M. Kravchinsky (Stepnyak)—Narodnik, the author's husband.—*Ed.*

There were heated arguments among the guests, who got excited, shouted, and asked Engels for the answer to the question.

Suddenly Engels turned to me and, taking into account the fact that I knew no foreign languages, spoke Russian. He quoted from Pushkin:

V

Мы все учились понемногу,
Чему-нибудь и как-нибудь,
Так воспитаньем, слава богу,
У нас не мудрено блеснуть.
Онегин был, по мненью многих
(Судей решительных и строгих),
Ученый малый, но педант.
Имел он счастливый талант
Без принужденья в разговоре
Коснуться до всего слегка,
С ученым видом знатока
Хранить молчанье в важном споре
И возбуждать улыбку дам
Огнем нежданных эпиграмм.

VI

Латынь из моды вышла ныне:
Так, если правду вам сказать,
Он знал довольно по латыни,
Чтоб эпиграфы разбирать,
Потолковать об Ювенале,
В конце письма поставить *vale*,
Да помнил, хоть не без греха,
Из Энеиды два стиха.
Он рыться не имел охоты
В хронологической пыли
Бытописания земли;
Но дней минувших анекдоты,
От Ромула до наших дней,
Хранил он в памяти своей.

VII

Высокой страсти не имея
Для звуков жизни не щадить,
Не мог он ямба от хорея,
Как мы ни бились, отличить.
Бранил Гомера, Феокрита;
Зато читал Адама Смита
И был глубокий эконом,
То есть умел судить о том,
Как государство богатеет,
И чем живет, и почему

Не нужно золота ему,
Когда *простой продукт* имеет.
Отец понять его не мог
И земли отдавал в залог.¹
―――
¹

V

Since but a random education
Is all they give us as a rule,
With us, to miss a reputation
For learning takes an utter fool.
The strict and never doubting many
Maintained the notion that Yevgeny
Was "quite a learned lad", you see,
But "with a turn for pedantry".
Our hero had the lucky talent
Of making witty repartees,
Of speaking with unwonted ease,
Of looking wise and keeping silent
And of provoking ladies' smiles
By unpremeditated guiles.

VI

None really care for Latin lately:
Our friend's sufficed him to translate,
Although not very adequately,
An epigraph, at any rate;
To say a word on Juvenale,
To wind a letter up with *Vale*
And cite, with just a slip or two,
A pair of Virgil's lines to you.
He had no itch to dig for glories
Deep in the dust that time has laid,
He let the classic laurel fade.
But all the most amusing stories
Of every century and clime
He could recall at any time.

VII

Unable to divine the pleasure
Of sacrificing life on rhyme,
He couldn't tell a single measure
However much we wasted time.
He chid Theocritus and Homer,
But might have won a Grand Diploma
For having tackled Adam Smith,
And knowing all the means wherewith
A state may prosper, what it needed
To live, and how it might abide
The lack of gold if it provide
Itself with *simple product*; heeded
He wasn't by his father, who
Mortgaged his lands without ado.

He recited the whole by heart in wonderful Russian. I clapped, but Engels said: "Alas, that's as far as my knowledge of Russian goes!"

The impression he produced on me was indelible, he was so hospitable and open-hearted. A few days later he returned our visit. He did not stay long, obviously merely wanting to make acquaintance. I never saw him again in a large company. He and my husband used to see each other and meet to talk about various political subjects; they sometimes had arguments and misunderstandings.

* * *

My attitude to Engels was perhaps a sentimental one and it was shared by Vera Zasulich, who was a friend of mine. She and I used to meet sometimes and when we spoke of Engels we were on the point of crying: Engels was very ill at the time.

Once Mrs. Kautsky came and said that she had to go somewhere and would I go to Engels for a couple of hours. I spent about three hours with Engels and the very sight of him hurt me. He was glad when he recognised me and he showed me all the armchairs on which Marx had ever sat. He also showed me letters from Karl Marx, his photographs and some caricatures of him. All this he did with the greatest warmth. And there was I, looking at him and suffering, for he had been so hale and hearty when I first met him and now he was ill and helpless. His disease was a dangerous one—cancer of the throat.

However, Engels kept up his interest in all events to the very end and wrote much. Vera Zasulich often went to see him and shared impressions with me. All those who loved him often visited him and spent hours with him, but all knew that he was doomed....

REQUEST TO READERS

Progress Publishers would be glad to have your opinion of this book, its translation and design and any suggestions you may have for future publications.

Please send your comments to 21, Zubovsky Boulevard, Moscow, U.S.S.R.